# Pastoral Care, Health, Healing, and Wholeness in African Contexts

# African Practical Theology

## BOOK SERIES INTRODUCTION

THE TASKS OF CHRISTIAN ministry in African contexts have most often proceeded through the ingenuity of African practitioners utilizing resources written for and from Euro-American contexts. In the main African Christian practitioners have had to adapt or contextualize such material to suit their immediate situation. The aim of the books in this *African Practical Theology* series is to provide relevant resources for pastors, faith community leaders, educators, and all others who influence Christian practice in African contexts written from a decidedly African perspective. Each of these texts draw specifically from three bodies of knowledge namely, theological, human scientific and contextual. The intention is to model the necessarily thoughtful, creative and faithful scholarship needed to inform Christian practice in African contexts.

By "African contexts" is meant not only the geographical continent of Africa but also the many spaces, places, and communities in Europe, the Americas, the Caribbean, and throughout the globe where persons of African descent gather for Christian nurture and practice.

Each volume is a collected set of essays authored by people of African descent domiciled in any of the aforementioned spaces whose concern, research and practice has a direct bearing on Christian practice in these locations.

Of great importance in this collection of works is the interdisciplinary dialog that has typically informed Christian practice historically as well as the mutually beneficial interactions that continue to take place between theory and practice, faith and experience, theology and life.

Our expectation is that these books will not only remain on the bookshelves of educated pastors and leaders but also that they will be consulted actively and constantly by practitioners in their daily exercise of ministry. Our hope is that they will assist in the refining of effective and fruitful ministry specifically in African contexts.

Emmanuel Lartey and Tapiwa Mucherera
General Editors

# Pastoral Care, Health, Healing, and Wholeness in African Contexts

*Methodology, Context, and Issues*

EDITED BY

TAPIWA N. MUCHERERA
AND EMMANUEL Y. LARTEY

WIPF & STOCK · Eugene, Oregon

PASTORAL CARE, HEALTH, HEALING, AND WHOLENESS IN AFRICAN CONTEXTS
Methodology, Context, and Issues

African Practical Theology, Vol. 1

Copyright © 2017 Tapiwa N. Mucherera and Emmanuel Y. Lartey. All rights reserved. Except for brief quotations in critical publications or reviews, no part of this book may be reproduced in any manner without prior written permission from the publisher. Write: Permissions, Wipf and Stock Publishers, 199 W. 8th Ave., Suite 3, Eugene, OR 97401.

Wipf & Stock
An Imprint of Wipf and Stock Publishers
199 W. 8th Ave., Suite 3
Eugene, OR 97401

www.wipfandstock.com

PAPERBACK ISBN: 978-1-4982-2188-7
HARDCOVER ISBN: 978-1-4982-2190-0
EBOOK ISBN: 978-1-4982-2189-4

Manufactured in the U.S.A.                              DECEMBER 16, 2016

# Contents

*Introduction by Emmanuel Y. Lartey* | *vii*

| | | |
|---|---|---|
| Chapter 1 | African Spirituality that Shapes the Concept of Ubuntu \| 1 *by M. J. S. Masango* | |
| Chapter 2 | Pastoral Authority and Responsibility \| 15 *by Esther E. Acolatse* | |
| Chapter 3 | Healing in Contemporary African Christian Contexts in the Face of the HIV & AIDS Pandemic \| 30 *by Tapiwa Mucherera* | |
| Chapter 4 | Conjunction of Gender Violence and HIV/AIDS with Implications for Assessment and Intervention in Pastoral Care \| 61 *by Anne K. Gatobu* | |
| Chapter 5 | Healing Postcolonial Trauma in the African Experience \| 76 *by M. Fulgence Nyengele* | |
| Chapter 6 | The Aftermath of Violence \| 99 *by Mazvita Maching* | |
| Chapter 7 | Deliverance and Delivery \| 114 *by Emmanuel Y. Lartey* | |

*Contributors* | *125*
*Bibliography* | *131*

# Introduction

MINISTRY IN POST-COLONIAL AFRICA and in the African diaspora throughout the world faces particular challenges, especially in this current geo-political and socio-economic climate. In spite of vast geographical, social, and historical differences, there appear to be several synergies and commonalities when it comes to cultural and experiential realities confronting people of African descent. African churches of the mainline denominations, including those dubbed "Black-majority" in Britain and "Black Church" in North America, share a common legacy of European colonial teaching. African Indigenous Churches ("Spiritual churches" in West Africa and "Prophet-Healing or Zion" churches in East, Central, and Southern Africa) occupy the position of seeking, in reaction to the Euro-Christianity of the mainline churches, to be more culturally embedded within their African cultural heritage. African Pentecostal and charismatic churches find their models mostly from the Mega-churches of North America, which hold a particular attraction for African–descended peoples because of the attention paid to their lived experiences and material circumstances. In all African churches there is evidence of conscious as well as unwitting influences, importations, and interactions with Western Christianity in many and various ways. However, what is shared goes far beyond western Christian teaching. In fact, arguably, it is African cultural heritage and African ways of being and thinking that loom largest in the set of influences Africans contend with and seek to live by. This pervasive "Africaness," though vaguely recognized, has seldom been taken into serious consideration in educating and providing resources for persons in ministry. The West has typically provided the concepts, models, and practices that have been most influential in ministry in African contexts.

This book is the first in a series on *African Practical Theology* that aims at providing resources for pastors, faith community leaders, educators, and others who influence Christian practice in African contexts from a decidedly African perspective. By "African contexts" is meant not only the geographical continent of Africa but also the many spaces, places, and communities in Europe, the Americas, the Caribbean, and throughout the globe where persons of African descent (whether historically through the iniquitous slave trade or more recently through migration) gather for Christian nurture and practice.

In Christian ministry and practice in these African contexts three bodies of accumulated knowledge are often recognized, namely Theology (including Bible, history, Christian teaching), Human Sciences (including sociology, psychology, health sciences), and Culture (including African beliefs, practices, traditions).

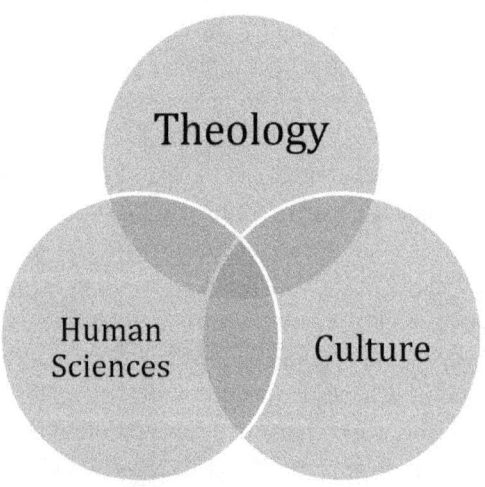

The authors of each of the chapters in this book draw from each of these three arenas in recognition of the fact that true and effective ministry happens at the intersection of the three. Stated otherwise, it is in the center of the above diagram, where these three forms of knowledge impact each other and interact together, that one finds ministry that addresses the needs and experiences of the people served. For truly meaningful ministry to happen persons-in-ministry need to take careful cognizance of each of these areas of knowledge. They need especially to bring them into critical, creative, and constructive dialog on any area or aspect of work they are engaged on. This is what each of the chapters of *Pastoral Care, Health, Healing, and Wholeness in African contexts*, attempts to do.

South African pastoral theologian, Maake Masango, of the University of Pretoria provides the first chapter in the book. In it he sets the conversations of this text in the wide frame of African spirituality, which in its holistic and communitarian frame is based upon and fueled by the personalist philosophy and understanding Ubuntu. Masango explores how African traditional society nurtures and socially transmits respect for personhood, the elderly, and the *sensus communis*, through the nurturing activities of parents and family. Village values lead African communities towards a global consciousness in which "I am because we are." African spirituality, Masango argues, reflects the wholeness of life and serves to harmonize all aspects of life into a fullness that transcends body, mind, soul, and society. Health and healing can and must be sought within this encompassing frame. But who is to provide the leadership for the cultivation of such healthy community? Dr Esther Acolatse, Ghanaian practical theologian and professor at Duke University, provides a critical response considering pastoral authority and leadership. Surveying various historic and contemporary models of leadership within ecclesial communities, she argues for responsible leadership that is informed by the checks and balances implicit within African traditional governance structures. When these are infused with and patterned after Biblical understandings of Divine authority and human responsibility, Acolatse inspires us to see how true Christian communities may be built up.

In the chapter that follows, Tapiwa Mucherera, pastoral care professor at Asbury Theological Seminary draws on his Zimbabwean roots and pastoral theological training to face squarely the challenges in the quest for healing in the face of HIV & AIDS. Mucherera's chapter examines and expands understandings of healing and points to the relevance and importance of social and communal relations in service, not merely of curing but rather of "wellness" in all its breadth. In a trenchant exploration of notions of 'confidentiality' as insisted upon from western perspectives, he succeeds in demonstrating how invasive, and indeed harmful, some of the best western concepts and practices can be if not interrogated contextually in healthcare settings. His chapter ends with a clarion call for non-abusive religious leadership that is courageous enough to dig deeply in both African heritage and Biblical literature for models and rituals of healing that may transform whole communities. Anne Gatobu, also an African professor writing from Asbury Theological Seminary, lifts up the stark realities of the gender divide when it comes to the African experience of HIV/AIDS. The figures are disturbing and the gender violence that ensures that women are disproportionally affected and infected is alarming. Gatobu gives voice to the excruciating pain of silenced women across sub-Saharan Africa. Her call for the empowerment of women from all sections of the African world sorely needs to be responded to.

The brutality and violence unleashed upon the peoples of Congo by Belgian and British colonialists provides the context for Fulgence Nyengele's examination of the harrowing experiences of Africans during and after colonial domination. Nyengele, pastoral theologian from Congo, carefully explores the multi-generational transmission of despotic tyranny and brutal traumatization of communities, which has been and continues to be the bitter experience of too many Africans. He lifts up contemporary understandings of trauma and its transmission and points towards how Congolese people–and all Africans for that matter–might find healing through naming, identifying, mourning, and interrupting transmission of violence and trauma.

The focal point of Zimbabwean psychotherapist Mazvita Machinga's work is on healing in the aftermath of violence. Drawing on the discourse of survivors of political violence, she presents a model that promotes understanding, care, empowerment, and restoration of human dignity for individuals as well as communities needed in all contexts where violence is rampant.

The final chapter addresses the increasingly practiced ministries of deliverance popularized by Pentecostal and charismatic church leaders globally. In this essay, Ghanaian pastoral theologian, Emmanuel Lartey draws on Biblical, psychotherapeutic, and African social anthropological sources in offering important guidelines for persons who practice exorcism and various ministries that seek to rid people of evil forces. Interrogating basic assumptions underlying this practice and with a desire for respectful pastoral ministry, the chapter offers ways forward that integrate theological, human scientific, and contextual cultural realities.

What you have in this book, then, is a resource of information and thoughtful guidance based on experience and practice that aims at pastoral care and healing relevant to the experiences in the contexts where African descended people live and work today.

Emmanuel Y. Lartey, PhD
L. Bevel Jones III Professor of Pastoral Theology, Care and Counseling
Candler School of Theology
Emory University

# Chapter 1

## African Spirituality that Shapes the Concept of Ubuntu

PROF. M. J. S. MASANGO
UNIVERSITY OF PRETORIA

"The spiritual life is the whole of one's life insofar as it is motivated and determined by the Holy Spirit, the spirit of Jesus."[1]

AFRICAN SPIRITUALITY SHAPES PERSONS in such a way that they grow into the concept of Ubuntu (humanness). In other words, an integrated African spirituality is a spirituality in which who we are, and what we do, are intimately related. The process of an African spiritualist is also developed within the village. Mbiti reminds us that, "It takes a whole village to raise a child."[2] In short, relationship is part of the development of African spirituality. In this chapter I shall be exploring how elders within the village become leaders, and towards the end of their life journey, how they become teachers and good ancestors, especially to the younger generation. It is important to note that those who are good (while living), and are able

---

1. Nolan, *Biblical Spirituality*, 7.
2. Mbiti, *Introduction to African Religion*, 23.

to pass their knowledge and wisdom to others, also become good ancestors when they die.

The great wonderful gift that God has given to people is the gift of life. We are, therefore, charged to manage and take care of our lives. In Africa, self-management is closely related to one's world. In other words, how one lives his or her life is part of the management of this gift. In short, self-management is all about the living of the highest quality of human life, as well as being able to enjoy life in a positive Ubuntu style. Bhengu had this to say about life lived within the style of Ubuntu:

> "The enjoyment of life implicates that a person is aware of the value which gives joy to life and how to pursue this, especially being the master of life, as a person in the milieu of community and society."[3]

The enjoyment of life is part of living as much as Ubuntu is part of humanity. In fact, one grows with the above concept from early childhood, especially in rural African villages. As people grow and relate to each other they are taught by the elderly to pass on what they learn to another person. This is the beginning of caring for each other. The notion of caring manifests itself in the respectful and humble way elders and superiors are greeted and addressed by young ones. This kind of Ubuntu is passed on from one generation to the other. It will not be wrong to say that a human being is nothing, but humanness or Umuntu (a Zulu word for a person) is shared by many African tribes. This concept is enhanced through the creation story in the Bible. In the story, human beings are created in the image and likeness of God. Genesis captures this beautifully:

> "So God created man (sic) in his own image, in the image of God he createdhim, male and female he created them."[4]

In an African village the image and likeness of God is revered, and when you add the concept of Ubuntu, you must also connect it to African spirituality, which forms values and good character in a person. Their concepts are part and parcel of humanity from the beginning of the creation story. For example, Hermes (from Egypt) wrote about these concepts, and Pythagoras continued writing and developing the ideas further as he studied in Africa. Later on, some of the African philosophers (Soclits and Onuphis) taught Hermes about the 'inner values and African concepts of humanness,' which

3. Bhengu, *Ubuntu*, 64.
4. Genesis 1:27.

were given to human beings by God. An African writer by the name of Koka connected the above ideas by developing the concept of respect and connecting the ideas to African spirituality. For example he says:

> "The word 'Ntate' (father) is used to address an old man or respectedfather figure in the village or community."[5]

When children or young ones call the word Ntate (father), they are showing a sign of respect to that adult person, and also see him as the one who shapes them into good citizens. As children continue to grow in the village, they are then shaped in respecting people, and the concept of Ubuntu becomes part of their life. Broodryk reminds us that:

> "Man (sic) was declared "Human" as soon as the element of "divine" (image) goodness (likeness) was instilled in him. This divine element that transformed man (matter) into a human being was nothing but a humanness, "ubuntu" that manifested the "Image and likeness" of God in each individual person of the human race."[6]

Broodryk points out that it was the spark of life that transformed human beings into living souls and made them different from the rest of created beings. Hence, we contain the main consistency of the wholeness of life. Once again he reminds us that this concept of Ubuntu was there from ancient times, and it never ceased to exist within the circle of the human race of well known ancient philosophers, who in turn were scholars of the Hermetic Philosophy, theology, and science. This was based on the "logos" (creative word) and the doctrine that was taught by the African priests of Hermes in Egypt. For example, Pythagoras was one of those who studied this concept for twenty-two years in the University of Heliopilis under two Egyptian high priests—Socht and Onuiphis. Their theory was centered around inner-value and dignity of the human personality which is nothing else but "humanness." The summary of their theory was further developed by Savory who finally said that:

> "God (supreme God) did not only endow man (sic) with his goodness" but also equally inseminated this divine element into all human beings."[7]

---

5. Koka, *Ubuntu*,13.
6. Broodryk, *Ubuntu*,1.
7. Savory, *The Best of African Folklore*, 29.

The above quotation reminds the author of the connection between creation (that is, image of God) and the gift of life (breath, breathed in all human beings), which brings us closer to the concept of Ubuntu, and that leads into deep African Spirituality. As beings we are always searching for a higher being. The question to ask is, what is African spirituality? Concept of African Spirituality has become a common word in modern life. Current interest in spirituality is evident both at popular and scholarly levels. This theme is heard from radios and televisions. These days it is also shared in Africa in seminars, conferences, universities, classes, course work, and curricula. Modern society is re-visiting this old concept once again in order to correct the values and dignity of Ubuntu that is lost. Why? South Africans lost their concept of Ubuntu during apartheid, when they fought for their liberation. During those days, life lost its meaning, especially the concept of the image and likeness of God, which kept them respecting each other. In the new democracy, with the emphasis on human dignity and human rights, the community is trying to recover old concepts that kept villagers and people respecting each other. The above has given us reason why we should re-evaluate or re-examine the concept of Ubuntu.

In the new democracy, people are in need of, or are searching for, a deeper meaning of life. The main question to ask is how the church or religious institutions can address the spiritual hunger that is experienced by the nation in South Africa. It is also important to note with interest that many African people are now tracing back their African roots. For example, after the 1976 riots, a lot of parents started naming as well as re-naming their children African names. They departed from naming and using English names. This concept is also seen in the changing of the names of cities such as Louis Trichard to Makhado, Pretoria to Tshwane, etc. Listening to the radio one could hear the efforts of whites who are also learning how to call or pronounce different African names while struggling during radio discussions. The above changes are examples of the shifting of old concepts, of western ways of thinking, into new African ways of life. On the other hand, the church is still struggling to address these issues of change. The struggles will continue as the new democracy grows. The result of these changes caused one of the Presbyterian churches to overture the General Assembly in 1999. The problems that they were seeking to address were on the subject of African spirituality and ancestor veneration. Our white members were questioning the above problem, especially the issue of cult and idolatry. They felt the church was too liberal and accepting of everything that was African. The debates were high as African people were trying to define ways of recapturing their Africanness. The question of African spirituality and ancestor veneration as a cult became a crucial topic for African delegates. African people centered their arguments on the respect of the dead. They argued that the respect of the dead was an important way of showing signs of respect to leaders who lived a good life. The argument was based on the concept of Ubuntu and not on ancestor worship. The African delegates found themselves caught in areas of dualism. This concept became part of their lives, because of Christianity. They found themselves practicing the African way of life, and also keeping Christian principles that were foreign and western.

The debates made them aware that there are some Africans who live western as well as the African way of life. Other Africans blamed colonialism for these two kinds of dualism. Those who favored Christianity as a way of life rejected those who practiced an African way of life. They referred to them as hedonistic or unchristian. In other words, Christians were seen as good people, and Africans as bad. This way of life continued to divide Africans into the two camps. History became an important way of arguing, especially regarding the concept of missionaries. For example, as missionaries continued to work among the Africans, the Africans had to leave their way of life and embrace western concepts of life as a good way of living. They also developed a process of dividing African graveyards into three parts: one for the Christians, one for non-Christians, and one for Catholic believers. This way of division further caused undermining among Christians and non-believers. For example, Christians saw themselves as righteous, while others were sinners. After the new democracy, that process was stopped. The above process caused some of the Africans to resort to their former African customs. Missionaries missed the point that the concept of ancestor relationship is not idolatry. They forgot the connection of respect of the dead and the notion of Ubuntu. There is a great belief among Africans that if a person lived a good life and dies (divine life), that person, according to African belief systems, becomes a good ancestor. He or she is able to connect one to higher powers (Jesus the King). In other words, that person is believed to be in heaven. The second belief is that the person is given to another world (eternal life), and hence, when they bury their loved one, they provide food and other important items that are buried with them. The final belief is that ordinary human beings cannot speak to God directly, because God is not their equal. Hence, ancestors become a bridge between the lower and higher being. The author is aware that Jesus is our mediator, who connects us-directly to God. I am merely stating the case of those who believe in the system of ancestorship. The above concept shares light into the way some Africans communicate, and thus, should not be taken lightly by those who do not operate in that world. As a strategy, understanding this could have been used in order to connect them with Christian belief systems.

The difficulty of some Africans speaking to a hierarchy is a problem in certain rural areas. They use a system of Induna's or mediators, especially when they speak to a king. That same process of communication was brought into Christian practices by some of them. They find it difficult to talk directly to a higher being without a spokesperson. When they share their problems they will always seek a mediator, because they feel that they are talking to someone who is not their equal. In other words, they will share their problems, happiness, and sadness, or any other difficulty via a mediator. The concept of hierarchy and authority comes into play whenever they feel the person to be higher in position. For example, when one connects the above process with the concept of Induna (spokesperson) or spiritual mediator, one will begin to understand the world of communication among African people. Mbiti reminds us that

> "The African view of the universe or the world, understands spiritual mediators as people who fill up the area between man (sic) and God."[8]

This concept can be a beautiful and beneficial contribution in understanding the world of communication among Africans, especially when introducing Christianity and the concept of Jesus as mediator. It could have helped them connect to the world of Jesus as Savior of the world, especially its process of hierarchy. That is, one can only speak to the king through a spokesperson, and in the case of Christianity, that spokesperson is Jesus. Returning to the concept of hierarchical structures (of African world ancestors), it makes sense that one can only speak to King (God) through ancestors or mediators, especially the good ones who lived life to the fullest. Only good role models are respected, especially those who have shared their good behavior with others in the village.

Let us now analyze the issue of death, which will help us to develop the concept of spirituality that leads to Ubuntu.

---

8. Mbiti, *Introduction to African Religion*, 76.

## DEATH OF GOOD ELDERS

Generally speaking, not everybody becomes an ancestor in the true African life. For example, those who lived bad lives can never be considered as ancestors when they die. In Africa, (as mentioned before) death does not represent the end of human existence, but rather a change in its status. The notion of death creates a solution of continuity between the living and the dead, a solution marked by the differences on the scale between the "creditors" (the dead) and those "debtors" (their heirs). Belief in the existence of spirituality or spirit is widespread throughout Africa. Mbiti continues to share the above idea by saying that:

> "It is a natural consequence of the strong belief in African religion that human life does not terminate at the death of the individual, but continues beyond death."[9]

It follows, therefore, that there must be myriads upon a myriad of human spirits. Many of them appear in legends, myths, and folks stories; others are spoken about in normal conversations among people; and some possess people, or appear to people in visions and dreams.

In other words, the African world has always been interacting between the world of the living and the dead. Note that the process begins even before the last breath of the elderly has been breathed out. We are now entering the area of deep human spirituality through the process of death. For example, in certain villages, elders become living ancestors as they reach the prime age in their lives. They become spiritual advisors to the young ones. This process starts when they are sharing their spiritual gifts or insights while they are still alive, and then proceed to do so when they pass on to the other life. At the point of death or passing to another world, some of the villagers believe that they (ancestors) share the image and likeness of God. In short, they are closer to God. Abimbola when sharing this idea of good ancestors says:

> "It is important to note that not all dead people automatically attain the status of ancestorship. Death is not always a requirement for it. . . . The notion of ancestorship implies the idea of selection, before any other consideration to a social model based on the idea of exemplification in the strictest sense of the word. . . . the good elder becomes an image of God when he (sic) dies."[10]

9. Mbiti, *Concepts of God in Africa*, 23.
10. Olupona, *African Spirituality*, 11.

Said another way, an ancestor is someone who has reached a great age and maturity in life, who, during his or her lifetime, has acquired a vast experience of life, including deep spirituality. Hence, they share their rich experiences and spiritual life with other young villagers. As mentioned before, this process starts in the prime of one's life while one is still alive. There are certain expectations required from a good elder, especially during their last stages of life. In short, his or her death must conform to the rules of the village or society to which he or she belongs. Awolalu[11] shared a good explanation on this issue of a death of an elder. He says:

> "Death by ill "reputed" diseases [such as leprosy] or by accident [especially if provoked by lightning] means exclusion from the village (society) of being an ancestor."[12]

The above quotations take seriously the steps of good position of ancestorship. It also shares a passage of ritual that leads one to becoming an ancestor. The requirements lead to a position of maturity in a good life that develops a deep spirituality in a life of an elder. That life plays an important part in forming a good person, especially towards entry into the world of ancestorship. In other words, living a good life, as well as sharing your values with others, creates a good personality that will remain within villagers even when you have died. A further explanation is that living a good life as well as sharing your good values with villagers, even when you have died, leaves good memories that are internalized and used when difficulties of life approach. During these times of struggle, one is able to use the wisdom shared by good ancestors. In short, the passing on of knowledge or wisdom creates a world of humanness (Ubuntu) among other people. The concept is further developed by a deep reverence or respect of the dead (ancestors) by villagers or African people. The above can be achieved by those who lived a good life that impacted those who remain. Other Africans believe is that the society of these gloriously dead represents a perfect community, unlike the society of the living, where one finds good and bad people, pure and impure people, handsome and ugly people, etc. The above world introduces one to a concept of dualism, which is only experienced by the living, while the dead, especially good ones, experience only goodness. Mbiti summarizes this by saying:

---

11. Cited in Olupona 1991.
12. Olupona, *African Traditional Religion*, 6.

"In the land of the dead, contradictions, tensions, oppositions are exempted."[13]

While Zahan[14] continues with the idea saying:

"The world of the ancestors is one that is free of antitheses and violence, because it resides in a slow time. Ancestors can, of course, become incensed and they are even susceptible to suffering."[15]

Returning to the overture of whites in the Presbyterian church before the Assembly, they understood the world of ancestorship as a cult or idolatry, and, thus, misunderstood the development of the spirituality that was connected to this concept, especially by those Africans who were Christians. If they understood this world of ancestorship and how it operates, they would not have addressed the General Assembly, because good ancestors are taken as people who are close to the Lord. Therefore, African people will always talk or communicate with them because of the heirarchial relationship. The Indunas or mediators (spokespersons) play an important part. With the above facts in mind, let us now analyze how African values connect and are shaped in the village or African community.

## AFRICAN VALUES

The concept of Ubuntu, connected to the idea of ancestorship shapes a way of living that respects human beings, life, the elderly, as well as the villagers (community). In this way, one is able to live with other people in a respectable way. It is a common saying among Africans, that it takes the whole village to raise a child. The statement captures good values, ethics, and spiritual development of a personis holistically taken. This type of process forces one to internalize African values as a way of life. In other words, in an African community a person is expected to be in relation with other people. That is why an adult is allowed to discipline any child who is out of step. It is part of shaping values, ethics, and the spiritual life of a child. In the African village, one is not allowed to live life alone, like an island. Mbiti emphasizes this point by reminding us that:

13. Mbiti, *African Religion and Philosophy*, 36.
14. Article cited in Olupona.
15. Olupona, *African Spirituality*, 11.

"An individual does not exist alone except corporately."[16]

In other words, a way of life [which the author calls spiritual life] is lived in a community with others. Donker on the other hand had this to say about individualism:

> "The individual is not a physical being, but a spiritual and divine individual, who lives with other human beings."[17]

It is interesting to note that in the world of Africans, the paternal (spiritual) and the godly (divine) attributes of the individual are fully explored within the community. It can never be lived alone. In South Africa, the Nguni tribe shares another element of life that shapes a human being, through a powerful proverb or idiom that says: Umuntu ngumuntu ngabantu. Meaning a person is a person because of other people.

In other words, you cannot live a life of your own; you need other people who will help you live life to the fullest. Growing up in the village, the author discovered and came to appreciate that he is a communal being who was, and is still, nurtured and shaped by the ethos of other villagers. In short, it took the whole village in order to formulate the authors' spiritual life. The English saying became a reality to the author when living with others: It says: "no man (sic) is an island." This process of African spirituality formed and continues to form the author's own moral, ethical, and spiritual world. The author is aware that in the Western world, people had to respect privacy and a space of an individual as well as other people. In an African village (community), one is surrounded by lots of people, tribes, and kinsmen and women. Another concept that continues to shape African spirituality and the values of a person is the rites of passage (initiation) in the context of transformation during the maturational process. This process encourages elderly people to share their experience with others at the initiation school. In short, the rites of passage such as circumcision, marriage, and burials are good opportunities to shape the process of growth that leads to socialization and the integration of a person or group who would live harmoniously with other people. Setiloane affirms the above facts by saying that:

---

16. Mbiti, *Concepts of God*, 109.
17. Donkor, *African Spirituality*, 8.

> "In the African community, it is the responsibility of adults to shape children, so that they may learn how to live with others in the community."[18]

The above statement is important because it emphasizes how a community of adults shapes, nurtures, and cares for the spiritual upliftment of young ones within a village. African people are, by nature, nurturing and caring people. They live in the company of others and share concepts of raising children together. Therefore, being in relation to others, or belonging, represents the essential characteristics of being truly human. Hence, they have no private faith and spirituality. In other words, their faith and spirituality is communal.

## CHALLENGES

With the above facts in mind, I need to share that the world has changed and continues to change in such a way that it challenges the above concept of Ubuntu. For example, we are experiencing violence and abuse within African communities. As African people faced the challenges of women and child abuse, they were forced to re-examine where the concept of Ubuntu broke down. In other words, they needed to analyze the way they were raising their children in theses modern times. In today's society, the question they needed to ask was, is the village failing or has it collapsed in its African structure of caring and nurturing children? They also needed to dig deep into their African concept of spirituality, checking whether it was helpful in building the nation to its original way of living and respecting each other as they did before. The above challenges of abuse and violence in South African society are deeply rooted in the yearning of understanding that they are in relation to other human beings. Pato is helpful in sharing the following insights about these new challenges.
He says:

> "These challenges help us to dig deep into African wisdom and spirituality. They also help us to re-examine our problems and then meet the challenges that fence us in South Africa."[19]

The above challenges introduce us to the world of globalization. Globalization and modernism present us with new challenges that force

18. Setiloane, *African Theology*, 13–16.
19. Kourie and Kretzschmar, *Christian Spirituality*, 96.

Africans to re-examine their faith and lifestyle. In the older days, African people worked closely to each other. Today, the African community is breaking down; hence, the problems of abuse and violence are emerging. African people need to examine and analyze the social structure of their communities i.e. tracing were the blockages or brokenness occurred, especially those of abuse and violence. These questions will also help them realize that their whole pattern of life, which was viewed as religious from birth up to death, is being challenged by globalization. Secularization is also changing these concepts of the whole process of African life, which was based on spirituality, From the beginning, when a child is born, named, going through circumcision, through confirmation to man or womanhood, and to marriage, work, dying, death, and burial, this is seen as going through challenges, even though the process is still viewed as sacred, developing one's spiritual personality. Through this process a lot is expected from the elders, especially in rural areas. Magasa is right by saying that:

> "As repositories of sacred traditions, the elders are bound by higher moral imperative to be accountable to the community and their eternal predecessors, i.e. the ancestors."[20]

These great expectations, not only from the community but also from the ancestral world, are enforced upon them because of communal life. These are also taught to children so that they grow with these concepts in mind. That is why people who have accumulated experience within the village are expected to pass them on to the next generation before their own deaths. This process of accountability is expected from all members of the community. If you follow it, you then qualify to be a good ancestor after death. On the other hand, those who have lived and led an unethical life on earth are pronounced guilty, and therefore excluded from ancestorhood at the time of death. In other words, they have misled others and did not play a prominent role in shaping spiritual personality. They were not accountable to community while alive. Olupona is right when he challenges elders:

> "Their challenge then is to build into the spirit of Ubuntu, a new dimension of Citizenship to villagers."[21]

The expectation from elders is to live a good live that will eventually influence others in order to develop their own spiritual personality and,

---

20. Mageza, *African Religion*, 55.
21. Olupona, *African Spirituality*, 8.

thus, become good citizens, good neighbors, as well as fellow kinsmen. As a result of the above changes and challenges, people in urban areas are in search of the missing link of their life as well as the spirit of Ubuntu, due to the new democracy. A lot of people emphasize the individual rights more than the communal rights. That spirit of living together is slipping away. Those who live in South Africa will understand why we are battling with the issue of crime, abuse, and violence. The new society has to deal with the question of how to return to the spirit of Ubuntu, and harness it for productivity and the competitive purpose of building the nation. As we cultivate this new spirit of Ubuntu, we need to harness it in order to manage the challenges of reconstruction and development.

The African spirituality that connects to the spirit of Ubuntu, will lead to teambuilding, which will help form new values that will shape a generation that will work for peace. Mbigi and Maree say that:

> "This spirit of Ubuntu will also help us to find a new identify which will transcend the ethnic divisions that haunt the African continent."[22]

As we strive towards unity, it is in the spirit of Ubuntu, with its emphasis on working together and respecting human dignity, that will help us find our way forward as a continent. After addressing these problems faced by the new generation, we can celebrate our global citizenship, where we can be both tribal and cosmopolitan.

## CONCLUSION

African spirituality is holistic and it impacts the whole of life. It is not considered as an individual affair, because it is expressed in all levels of society: socially, economically, politically, as well as among people. Hence, it contributes in the building of a nation. Pato identifies it in the following way:

> "African spirituality is identified as reflecting the wholeness of life and is important in harmonizing life in all its fullness."[23]

In short, African spirituality has to do with the concept of nation building and the integrity of creation. In that life, everyone is involved in

---

22. Mbigi and Maree, *Ubuntu*, 9.
23. Kourie and Kretzschmar, *Christian Spirituality*, 3.

rebuilding spirituality in the lives of others. Ancestors are also involved in this process, as Kappen further says:

> "Contemporary spirituality impacts on the totality of life, it is non-dualistic, it does not posit a bifurcation between the secular and the sacred. It encompasses the entire life of faith, which includes body, mind, (and soul), as well as the social and political dimensions."[24]

The concept of body, mind, and soul also includes issues of ecology. This issue is an important part of life, especially in the way Africans relate to nature. The above highlights the concept of spirituality, which is ecological, manifesting sensitivity towards and solidarity with the earth. Africans regard Mother Nature not as an object of subjugation, but as a mother and symbol of the divine. In the olden days, Africans would not cut a tree without certain rituals. People were connected to nature. The connection with the whole of nature was, therefore, important, nurturing it instead of dominating it. In conclusion, life in an African village is connected to the entire God created part of life. In other words, Africans are connected to God as much as creation is part of God. We are, therefore, charged to care for it. We need to go back to basics, the spirit of Ubuntu.

---

24. Kappen, *Spirituality In The New Age*, 33.

# Chapter 2

## Pastoral Authority and Responsibility
### *An African Traditional Leadership Model for Church Governance and Functioning*

ESTHER E. ACOLATSE
DUKE UNIVERSITY

THE ISSUE OF AUTHORITY is intertwined with the vocation of pastor. Whether in the appropriation, misappropriation, or denial of it, as when one sidesteps leadership in any given role, authority is a given. This is because authority derives from other than the person of the pastor. It is part of the call and the gift of ministry. Thinking of it as part of the person of the pastor is often what leads to its misunderstanding and results in its misuses. Misuse can occur either through authoritarian, autocratic, directive approaches to the care of the congregation—often in overt or covert abuse of power—or can be found in its obverse when pastors shirk proper leadership by failing to create and keep appropriate boundaries between their leadership function as pastor and their personal life. Pastors caught in this latter category of misuse of authority are often women who are usually correcting for what they assume to be the male perspective, which is seen as hierarchical and autocratic. Either stand, however, affects the tenor of the congregation and, thus, its health and wholeness. Furthermore, the real character of the church as salt and light in the world is diminished, and it is no longer a place where the Spirit of truth dwells and where people are led into the truth and can speak truth to one another. In short, it misses the hallmark of a fully alive church in which members live with integrity, a place where difference and disagreements are welcomed and are not the basis of disunity and fracture; that is, a real rather than a *faux* or pseudo community.[1] Such an ecclesial space allows each member to flourish by receiving and giving his or her gifts without inhibition and or exhibition. But this kind of atmosphere has to be intentionally cultivated. Unfortunately, however, churches give a lot of attention to their physical architecture and geography, which is not bad in itself, but what is needed more is attention to their emotional geography and architecture. Much of a church's emotional health depends on leadership and especially that of the pastor or head pastor, as the case may be, in larger congregations.

## CONTOURS OF LEADERSHIP AND AUTHORITY IN AFRICAN PASTORAL PRACTICE

Leadership and authority is a complicated issue in even advanced democratic societies, but in Africa (with resistant patriarchal structures and hierarchical social existence compounded by residual colonial oppressive systems) the church, which is to be an egalitarian communal space, flounders on the threshold of true equality, albeit within ordered church polity. Ultimately, in the church the buck stops with pastors and their understanding of authority. In the African context, in my view, understanding of ecclesial authority derives partly from the structures outlined above but also from a misconstruing and misappropriation of African traditional leadership models, particularly those of chieftains. Here the assumption is that the chief wields ultimate power in and of himself, as if the authority were intrinsic to his person and his status, rather than as a function of the office to which he is appointed. Moreover, in the same vein, it seems that African pastoral leadership largely acts as if unlimited power is conferred on the pastor. But that is not the case. If it can be shown that traditional African chieftaincy structures are not as authoritarian/autocratic as assumed, if we can come to the knowledge that checks and balances are woven within its fabric for the welfare of the stool (the seat of traditional government) as

---

1. In the latter communities, members are not allowed to disagree, especially with the leadership, let alone the group, and are at the risk of being ostracized if they step out of the dictates of the group. Kornfeld, *Cultivating Wholeness*, 18–32.

well as for the nation state,[2] perhaps it can become an avenue for developing a better model of pastoral leadership for African churches. Further, if this nuanced African chieftaincy model is juxtaposed with biblical understandings of apostolic authority; we may find a comprehensive model for leadership that is conducive to the African context and ecclesial space. The church will become a wellspring that sustains all people, especially the most vulnerable, which continues to be women and children.

In this reflection on pastoral authority, I begin with a synopsis of church and leadership functioning in representative churches in the African context. This is followed by an exploration of the dynamics of African Traditional leadership with particular attention to traditional leadership in the Ghanaian context. I intend to use the insights from chieftaincy, through the ordering in military ranks to priestly office as representative of what pertains in various forms across the continent.[3] I then trace the contours of leadership among God's people as portrayed in the Old and New Testaments and compare them with those of traditional African leadership styles from which contemporary churches are, by and large, moving away. I conclude by making a modest proposal for a leadership model that entails an intricate balance of power between shepherd/pastor and sheep/congregation that allows all to flourish.

---

2. I would argue that it is in fact Western missionary enterprises, in collusion with colonial administrators with their European expansionist agenda, which are the culprits of the new mode of understanding leadership pervading the Government and church administration in Africa. As Opoku notes, part of the problem lay with the false assumption that the African was childlike and incapable of self-government despite the fact that several policies of indirect rule could only have been possible with a people in a stable society—a stability indicative of self-government. Even in egalitarian Christian community, the African was seen and engaged as a younger brother, in relation to his older brother, the European. Opoku, "The West Through African Eyes," 44–79.

3. The vastness of the continent and the various nations and even ethnic groups notwithstanding, there is a commonality among cultural norms around chieftaincy and leadership that can be recognized continent-wide and especially in Sub-Saharan expressions. See Dickson, *Theology in Africa*, for an extended discussion about differences and also similarities based in shared history and cultural norms. However, this point is somewhat in tension with the views of Kwame Anthony Appiah.

## A SNAPSHOT OF PASTORAL LEADERSHIP IN SOME REPRESENTATIVE DENOMINATIONS

Leadership in the Christian community, in particular the relationship between ordained and lay persons, is not uniform across denominations. Frequently, various forms of hierarchical functioning are found, and in a way that raises questions about the reformed understanding of the priesthood of all believers—an understanding that undergirds how I am reading and responding to what I see as the issues of pastoral authority in the African context. In Reformed thought, since all Christians expect, as a result of their baptism and calling, to die daily to self in service to God and the world, all are considered priests by virtue of this sacrifice; all are indeed called to service of Word and Sacrament. But if all Christians preached and celebrated the sacraments within any one particular church, as Luther notes, there would be chaos; hence, the specifying of certain ordained tasks for the pastor.[4] In large part then, assigning ordination to some is primarily for the purpose of order and organized ecclesial function. Though the current leadership style and its effects vary across denominations and, perhaps even more so across geographic/national lines, it is arguable that the biblical concept and Reformed emphasis on the "priesthood of all believers" and the fact that the ordained minister comes from among the people they serve, is often lost on pastors. Additionally, the laity themselves contribute to the wide gap between the ordained and lay members that exists especially in the African church today. The special place of honor given to 'people of the cloth' in public spaces, as well as the reverence and deference accorded them, all add to the tendency to equate the clerical office with the person of the minister. Today it is more important than ever to address the issue of pastoral authority, not only because of its effect in the church but also because it affects what goes on in the public square. This is especially true in Africa, where the voice of the pastor—or in more recent times that of the "prophet"—permeates the political and social life.[5]

In West Africa, an area with which I am most familiar, it is fair to state that one can observe various levels of leadership function across the denominations that can be grouped into Mainline, African Initiated Churches, Bible Churches, and various Interdenominational Churches,

---

4. Ellingsen, "Luther's concept of the Ministry," 338–46.

5. Marshall, *Political Spiritualties*, and Wariboko, *Nigerian Pentecostalism*, the latter offers a more optimistic account of Pentecostalism and its ethos in spite of the drawbacks of some of the leadership in Africa.

Pentecostal and Apostolic Churches, and the newer Evangelical/Charismatic churches, which follow mainly the American Prosperity Gospel ethos in worship and leadership. What does current leadership style and its effects in the various denominations in our current ecclesial spaces look like and what do they represent?

## MAINLINE OR HISTORIC CHURCHES

In the mainline churches, largely founded in the mid to late nineteenth century by Anglican, Methodist, and Presbyterian missionaries from Europe and later by Baptists, denominational governance and leadership selection processes are guided by polity. There are rules for upper and middle governing bodies and for the ordination of ministers for pastoral office, including theological training in accredited tertiary institutions and seminaries. To a large extent, leadership in these churches tends to be more democratic, and in some like the Baptist churches the Board of Deacons wields extensive power in the daily life and ministry of the church and also over the pastoral staff. Yet, even in these churches with seeming shared governance, there is the tendency on the part of congregants to invest the pastoral office with so much power because of the esteem in which the ministers are held continent-wide. The history of election to church office in Africa has many untold stories of power grabs, as well as various forms of canvasing and political posturing for positions of Moderator and Bishop. That, in spite of the denominational polity to guide deliberations, jockeying for power continues and relinquishing leadership is excessively difficult for outgoing leaders are further proof of the misunderstanding and misuse of authority to which I refer. If churches do not split over the choice of leader because of this misuse of authority, at the very least a divisive spirit is often left in its wake. While it is clear that Middle and Upper Governing[6] positions are coveted and sought among ministers, the reason may lie in more than the person seeking power. It is possible, I believe, to ascribe the desire for powerful positions in the church to a projection by the laity onto these Christian ministers, the power and awe vested in the office of the traditional priesthood as mediator between the gods and the people. I will return to a deeper exploration of this concept in the course of the paper.

---

6. This would be the leadership at the national, regional/district levels respectively. For example in the Presbyterian Church one could think in terms of the Moderator of the Synod and the Synod Clerk; the Chairpersons and District Clerks respectively.

## LEADERSHIP IN THE AFRICAN INDEPENDENT CHURCHES

African Initiated Churches (AIC) came into being after the mission churches failed to fulfill the spiritual needs of Africans who wished to worship as Africans. Many started as breakaway groups from the mainline denominations. In the words of John Pobee, there was the need for the African to seek a worship space in which "to feel at home."[7] These were churches characterized mainly by African liturgical styles in ritual and dress and sometimes were not devoid of traditional sacrificial rites and, in large part, as Pobee notes, functioned as a second tribe for their members.[8] A typical example is the Holy Apostles of Aiyetoro in Nigeria or the Apostles Revelation Society, founded in Ghana, where the lines between what is practiced in the African Traditional Worship space and that of the church are often crossed.[9] Here leadership often bears the markers I alluded to earlier: the pastor seems to replace Christ and mediates between the people and God in covert and sometimes overt ways. It is not unusual to actually refer to pastoral encounters as "consultations"—a word that evokes the kind of power-distance between laity and the minister. A word, I must add, which is also used in the traditional domain with the same connotations, whether it be in reference to encounters with a medicine man, a shrine, or the traditional ruler. In short, the authority of the pastoral role here is almost all encompassing and the pastor becomes mediator between the people and God.

## EVANGELICAL CHARISMATIC/PENTECOSTAL/APOSTOLIC

Many of the churches in the first set of this group, the Evangelical Charismatic, were founded by the current leaders who started off as pastors and then became head pastors and eventually rose to the office of Archbishop with the growth and expansion of their churches. Often in these churches,

---

7. Pobee, "African Instituted."
8. Ibid.
9. For instance, the worship in the Apostles Revelation Society is based primarily on Old Testament forms and, beyond the mandated bare-footedness in worship, included animal sacrifice to bring cleansing to individuals and the society. Such practices brought the Society into conflict with the Evangelical Presbyterian Church, with which it was briefly associated in the initial stages of becoming a church, and which now has congregations worldwide.

the leadership is very hierarchical and there is no accountability to any governing body as such since the churches are not connectional churches (as is the case with the mainline churches), and therefore do not all have a body that oversees their corporate functioning.[10] The fact that leadership and authority and sometimes power are conflated and seen as residing in these ministers is evidenced by not only the billboards with their pictures (often including their wives) displayed above the name of the church they lead, but also the relationship between the Archbishop and other ministers and the laity. In recent times some of these leaders have taken on the life style of "the rich and famous" and have bodyguards to protect them from the congregants as they enter and exit the worship space.[11] Here we see not only traces of the traditional leadership styles (that will be explored further) but also a Western display of wealth and prestige that suggests the church, in large part, has misunderstood what it means for the minister to be given authority by Christ. Additionally, the church has forgotten what it means to be a priesthood of believers[12] to lead together and serve one another. The church has missed, in a deeper sense, the true meaning of ordination and the transfer of apostolic authority via Christ to all believers and not just in the catholic sense of that which is handed through Peter to the heads of the church in time. Somehow these newer churches that distance themselves in polity and even theology from Mainline, and especially the Roman Catholic churches, are demonstrating a penchant for hierarchical ordering in their governance structure, not to mention their clerical garbs. They seem to have returned to a more papist stance with an autocracy that

---

10. Currently many of the Pentecostal/ Charismatic churches in Ghana belong to the Ghana Pentecostal Council (GPC) or the National Association of Charismatic and Christian Churches (NACCC)—bodies that provide oversight of conduct and ethical guidelines but no strict polity in any formal sense for governance in the individual churches. This is largely because the terms Pentecostal and charismatic in many instances are interchangeable and it is easy to find churches designated as Independent Charismatic in the GPC. See Amanor "Pentecostalism in Ghana," for a fuller account of the structures and parameters of membership in these two bodies.

11. I recall a recent incident in December 2013 on the way to a wedding in which we had to stop for a motorcade to overtake us on the road. My traveling companions and I later found out the motorcade was escorting an Archbishop who was apparently the officiant at the wedding.

12. I am aware that denominations differ on how they understand and live this concept but the evangelical/Bible-based tag placed on these churches warrants the point made here.

entrenches leaders in office until death, even as African chiefs stay in power until they die and are succeeded by other elected royals.[13]

What is worrisome about the leadership style is the often overt abuse of parishioners and care seekers through fear mongering, but also through physical abuse. Cases like that of the South African pastor who had his congregation go out and eat grass like cattle,[14] or the Kenyan Pastor who demanded women in the congregation desist from wearing underpants for worship in order that Jesus might enter them fully,[15] or the Ghanaian pastor who steps on the stomach of a pregnant woman to cure her of an affliction[16] all under the direct gaze of the congregation, may be sensational. But they also point to the extreme abuse of power often conflated with authority in the church today. It is shameful that the outcry from the public against such practices is louder than that which comes from the church, a further indication of the high esteem in which congregations hold their pastors. What is often missed by the churches in this group is that at base it a collection of people who, scripturally speaking, can hardly be termed church. Sermons, if they can be so described, and the style of delivery, mimic motivational speeches that are only somewhat informed by scripture. The business style/CEO model of its various heads further indicates what is amiss with leadership, especially one with hardly any accountability to the members of the church.[17] The questions that need to be asked and addressed before a valuable contribution can be made to the churches in this category are: (1) What exactly is the basis of what the church does and how can the church be distinct from any other social body? (2) How is a church both like and unlike other social bodies? Keeping a tight distinction between the callings of the church as *a particular* body birthed of God, grounded in the Holy Spirit, and brought daily under the scrutiny of God and the world to which God is sending the church is key to properly framing leadership. In

---

13. It is this same kind of understanding that seems to govern certain presidents of African countries who must be in power until they die and then, as in Togo, pass the seat to their heir.

14. "South African Pastor."

15. "Pastor Orders Women to Strip."

16. "Ghanaian Pastor Kicks."

17. More troubling in the church is the combination of the business model that is counterintuitive to the servant leadership model set up by Christ, a model in which sheep and shepherd are accountable to Christ and to one another and the greatest is the least. See Jackson, *God's Potters*, for a fuller dimension of the dangers and shortcomings of the business CEO model of church leadership.

other words, the church needs to clarify its identity in order to properly understand its function, for identity always precedes function. To rush into performing its function without understanding its identity and coming to terms with all that it involves produces mere show and performs a caricature of Christianity. In effect the very function, which is placed ahead of its identity, is derailed because it has missed attending to its identity as a "provisional demonstration of the Kingdom,"[18] a situation that can be attested continent-wide in many of our churches since the turn of the last century.

## LEADERSHIP IN THE APOSTOLIC CHURCH AND CHURCH OF PENTECOST

The Apostolic and Pentecostal churches are grouped together for convenience though there are serious enough doctrinal differences between them. For while the former is clearly Trinitarian, albeit with emphasis on the role of the Third Person, the later seems to be more Unitarian in its theology since it holds on to the idea of the oneness of God.[19] Clear role expectations may be gradually giving way to what may appear to be greater egalitarianism in the community, but by and large the churches in these two denominations work on a hierarchical model, which they believe is inscribed in the scriptures and which does not allow women to function in authority over men in the church. This means that women may lead and teach younger people and other women, but not men. Authority is still assumed to be tied to the male gender and residing in particular bodies, and it is assumed that power cannot be shared with those who traditionally play subordinate roles in the culture. The collusion of biblical, especially New Testament, household codes, with the African culture is most noticeable in these churches.[20]

---

18. The Presbyterian Church (USA) Book of Order describes the church and invites it to claim or live into its identity as a provisional demonstration of what God is about to usher in as the kingdom epitomized in the last two books of the Bible: A reconciled reconciling church with God as its center and in which all peoples find their being.

19. This essay is not the place to hash out deeper implications of the Pentecostal position on the Godhead—a position that separates Pentecostals from the evangelical mainstream. But their emphasis on the modesty of women as the foundation of holiness leads to a kind of policing of appearance that can border on the abusive.

20. This is not to indicate the absence of the reach of patriarchy, or the deep hierarchical foundations of African culture, despite the strides women have made in all spheres of life.

## LEADERSHIP, AUTHORITY, AND POWER IN AFRICAN CULTURE

I have made reference to two major contributing factors that are linked as possible causes of the misunderstanding and abuse/misuse of pastoral authority in the African context. Let me now offer an elaboration and analysis of this two-pronged cause.

African traditional relationships are built on groups with clearly identifiable leaders and clear roles for the leaders and those for whom they are responsible. This stretches from the father in charge of the smallest unit of the immediate family, the family head in charge of the extended family, through the clan with its titular head to the Chief of the tribe who might be a sub-divisional chief under authority to the Paramount Chief of a particular traditional area or region. What comes to the fore when one observes traditional African societies and how these various moving parts interrelate and function, each in its sphere and across all the discreet social structures, is the dynamic understanding of authority, albeit within strict role expectations. So for instance, though the chief has to come from the royal family and be vetted and approved by the *Ohemma*—Queen mother who is also the traditional kingmaker—he nevertheless goes through a strict search and selection process. Additionally, he must be subject to certain rituals and customary practices in order to be deemed fit to ascend to the throne and wield the power conferred on him through inheritance. There is no doubt that a deep spiritual ethos attends king-making because of the link between religion and culture in African society,[21] and the long line of succession based on the spiritual link between the stool and the office that confers certain spiritual properties to the new chief since departed chiefs are ancestors of the community. Yet, there are checks and balances in how the chief operates vis-à-vis the community, mediated by the council of elders.

There is a buffer between the populace and the possibility of autocratic rule and the danger of abuse of power. In fact, the kind of despotic rulers that Africa has experienced since independence from colonial rule could be attributed to the failure to include the traditional checks and balances in new nation states. Traditional familial relationships and governance, despite their patriarchal elements, nevertheless ensured care to all. Even the very name of "chief" in the Ga traditional understanding, "Maŋtse"—the father (*tse*) of the nation/state (*Maŋ*)—underscores this view: the functions

---

21. Busia, *The Position of the Chief*.

of protector and provider being integral to the father in this sense. Thus, while the populace looks up to the chief, it is a mutual relationship in which honor is bestowed on one who functions as such and who, thus, earns this respect. The oath *atamkese* sworn by the Ashanti chief on his enstoolment has the same mutuality of authority as a gift simultaneously conferred and received:

> I am the grandson of Osei and Poku
> I am the grandson of Nana Bonsu
> I am the grandson of Nana Agyeman
> Nana Kwame Kyiretwie was my uncle
> Opoku Ware II was my senior brother
>
> Today my elder brother Opoku Ware is gone to his village[22] and if by the grace of Kumasi people you have given his gun to me to rule, if I do not rule well, if I do not govern the state and protect you well as my forefathers did, I violate the great oath.[23]

The incumbent makes this pronouncement under the scrutiny of the Queenmother and the King's aunt who, in their physical and symbolic role, flank him. The two women sit high enough to be visible to the public and carry long chewing sticks in their mouths. Their presence and action indicates the kind of checks and balances of royal authority, for these sticks are also used in disciplining bad children. In other words, the king in authority is also under authority. To speak of discipline is to infer that when it fails, the king can be destooled or deposed. The adage "the king does no wrong" goes only so far in the African context and, when allegations against him can be sustained, then a process of destoolment and deposition, which are already laid down within the customary law, is set in motion so that removal is done efficaciously and collegially. This allows the stool—owners and occupants—to continue to maintain law and order in the area. And yet, as Kludze—writing about chieftaincy among the Ewe—notes, the counselors to the stool have a vested interest in the decision about destoolment since they are also advisors to the chief and may be hesitant in concurring readily.[24] Secondly, and closely tied to the role of king, is the idea of succession and their interrelation with enstoolment[25] and the psychospiritual

---

22. Reference to the land of the dead, the other-world from whence all people come.
23. "Installation of an Asantehene."
24. Kodzo and Kludze, *Chieftaincy in Ghana*, 302-303.
25. Here I am following Gry Osnes' in his article, "Succession and authority," 185-201.

attendants, which is understood among a people. Succession is a passing down of roles rather than status: it is assuming a role that eventually must be relinquished. This fact is of special relevance to how we should see the pastoral role, and has perhaps even greater significance given that the pastor is occupying a role seemingly occupied and vacated by the Good Shepherd. Biblical and African Traditional Concepts of Authority: Implications for the Church

A close look at the grounds and parameters of public leadership in both the church and African culture show marked similarities. Both priestly and kingly leadership require a definite provable line of succession. Additionally, the concept of chieftaincy described above demonstrates close links to the biblical notion of ministerial authority. Inscribed in the words of the vow of the chief, for example, are concrete references to past chiefs and the relationship of the new chief to the previous ones in the long line of succession. Apostolic understanding of pastoral authority and that of chieftaincy thus have the same basic notable assumptions. Inheritance is by bloodline and all within the bloodline are to a certain degree qualified for chieftaincy, and in the Christian religio-cultural sphere that means *all*. Moreover, the roles of priest and king co-inhere in the Christian and are a gift of adoption. The scriptures underscore this fact when they call Christians "a royal priesthood" (1 Pet. 2:9). It means at the least that all pastors are potential sheep and vice versa.

There is a subtle and yet distinct difference in how inheritance and succession evolves in the traditional understanding with regards to royalty and priesthood. There are strict guidelines in the selection process for both offices. Yet, while royalty is conferred by bloodline, priesthood in a sense is more than that. It is conferred but there is an additional qualification for it that transcends strict earthly bounds. Priesthood (in the traditional and also in the Christian sense) is an office that God or the gods chose even though it might pass through the bloodline. In other words, *Wonntsebi* (the progeny of a priest) do not necessarily become a *Wontse* (priest) in the traditional religious sense. Thus, there is room for the possibility that people could be passed over for the function of priesthood even if they are direct

---

He explores the idea of succession and role, built on the work of Boalt Boethius in which succession is conceived as "a phenomenon in which another enters a role that someone else is vacating, and where 'role' means not only the formal position but also the roles informally expected by the system". Further not only is the role the way in which the "the individual engages with and within organizations. . . . " but how to think of the individual as part of the system and yet apart and interacting with the system at the same time.

descendants of a priestly family. One has to be called, usually through possession by the god, often in utero, to qualify for the priesthood. Finally, those called and set aside for such offices, which also include the military, in the traditional setting are trained rigorously for this high office. Set rituals and designated elders assigned for such training and public displays of prowess, especially in the case of the priesthood and the military, are prerequisite for final approval and installation to the office. Call, attested to by the people, is needed for the public role of priest.

## BIBLICAL AND TRADITIONAL MODELS OF LEADERSHIP

### A Synthesis for Care in the African Church

It is clear from the above explorations that while there are areas of overlap between the African traditional understanding of leadership and inherent authority, care needs to be taken to distinguish "power" and in that of the scriptures. The biblical foundations for what the identity and formation of the pastor—the custodians of the soul—should be are exemplified first in God's life with Israel as shepherd and guide and then, as Israel settled into becoming a nation state, in the more structured set up of the priesthood. The priests were first and foremost a set of people who came from *among* the people since they were part of the twelve tribes. These were the Levites set aside for the priestly function and who were given appropriate training and strict instruction regarding their duties (Lev. 8-10) and life with the rest of the people, as well as education about their own fallibility and the need for confession and forgiveness. For this reason, there was always a forward look toward a better priesthood (Heb. 7-10). When these priests would misuse their power from time to time, the prophets would bemoan what they witnessed and warn them about their evil practices, suggesting that there were specific ways of being with the people and that these customary modes of interacting had been flouted time and again. A clear example of this misuse of power is noted as far back as the days of Eli's children, Hophni and Phinehas (1 Sam 2:12–36). By their behavior, they were disrespectful of God and the people by disregard for the holy things of God and their inability to place the needs of the people before their own selfish desires.

Similarly, in the New Testament Jesus ensures that church leadership, to which one is called and appointed, is stripped of brute power and the tendency to lord it over people. This is demonstrated by his own example made explicit in the foot washing before his death (John 13:1–17), as well as what Jesus expected of his disciples and later leaders of the church as suggested by key scriptures on authority and pastoral identity—as seen in Luke 10 and the sending of the seventy, and in the post-resurrection scene where Peter is commissioned by Jesus for ministry (John 22:15–18). The hallmark of both of these commissioning moments is the stripping off of masculine strength and the need for vulnerability, especially in the Lucan passage, as prerequisites for would-be followers and leaders of the church—workers in the vineyard. As Masiiwa Ragies Gunda notes in his exegesis of Luke 10, "Jesus challenges hegemonic masculinity of his day and asserts an alternative masculinity, which set his followers apart."[26] They were to go out not as 'manly men,' but as lambs among wolves with nothing but His peace for their anchor.

The whole mission . . . is predicated on goodwill and good faith on the part of the hosts of these men . . . they will have to be dependent in this journey, yet dependence is unmanly, the mission seeks to disabuse them from the populist understanding of manhood . . .[27]

The point clearly is that commissioning is for leadership and for work in God's vineyard and requires a lowly disposition, which God ensures by command and example. The incarnation, as well as Jesus' own ministry and life among the people and disciples and finally death on the cross, underscore this way of the Christian leadership. To lead in such a space is to receive one's authority from above; to be vulnerable is to honor God's standards rather than the socio-temporal standards of greatness. Perhaps the child who sits at the foot of the Ashanti Kings, depicting the King's soul, most typifies this essence.

## CONCLUSION

The conflation of authority and power observed in certain presidents of African nations and in leaders of some churches in Africa is a problem. Additionally, the insistence of current clergy and modern day 'prophets' that they cannot be disciplined or even corrected because they are anointed

26. Gunda, *Jesus Christ*, 16–33.
27. Ibid., 10 (italics original).

by God for office, needs to be challenged and addressed. This can be done on both traditional and biblical grounds. First, a return to the traditional African understanding of the role of the leader can offer a better set of ethics for leadership, and second, this can be coupled with a biblically informed foundation of pastoral leadership. Both the prophets in the Old Testament and Jesus, through the incarnation and instructions to his disciples, offer models to ameliorate what seems to be leadership run amuck in the churches in Africa today. In the end, we will have churches that are real Christian communities—spaces where people can be challenged by the scriptures and one another to do good works and to truly follow Christ.

# Chapter 3

## Healing in Contemporary African Christian Contexts in the Face of the HIV & AIDS Pandemic

### Dr. Tapiwa Mucherera
#### Asbury Theological Seminary

THE WORD HEALING HAS many connotations or interpretations. Healing is one of those words that can be used loosely depending on the context. Many people use the word to describe a cure from a physical ailment, while others use it to refer to a psychological or spiritual transformation that can occur with an individual. Yet, others use the word to refer to a total alleviation of suffering, physically, spiritually, socially, mentally, and/or emotionally.

This chapter starts with a socio-religio-historical quick survey of the beliefs about, and/or the understanding of, healing from the traditional to modern day sub-Saharan African contexts. Some materials from the Judeo-Christian traditions will also be used, especially the healing ministry of Christ. The similarities of symbolic actions, ritual practices, and the centrality of community, in both the African context and Jesus' healing ministry, will be noted. Given this background, the discussion will explore a two-prong understanding of African Christian perspective on healing in modern day sub-Saharan Africa in the age of HIV & AIDS, complicated by the introduction of the policies of confidentiality in communally oriented societies. In other words, the goal of this chapter is to do a quick survey of the meaning of healing in the African context, in the light of HIV and AIDS pandemic. The discussion will utilize materials from some of Christ's ministry and traditional African understanding, and will examine how these practices could be integrated and utilized in today's contemporary Africa. Implications to healing ministry in these African contexts will then conclude this discussion.

## A TRADITIONAL AFRICAN WORLDVIEWS ABOUT HEALING

Bojuwoye says the following about healing and its origins and development in Southern Africa, which still holds true to most contemporary African contexts today:

> The root of traditional healing among the people of Southern Africa today can be traced back to the time when the foundations of the cultures were being laid. The development of systems to respond to disease and restore health to individuals who are ill can certainly not be separated from the social cultural and historical contexts in which they occur. Traditional healing, as an integral part of culture, represents a sum total of beliefs, attitudes, customs, methods, and established practices indicative of the worldview of the people.[1]

The point that Bojuwoye is making in the above paragraph is that healing practices, beliefs, and methods are contextual. These practices and beliefs develop overtime and have been passed on from generation to generation.

Kamwaria and Katola in reporting about their research findings post war in Southern Sudan say the following about the Dinka (African) people's understanding about healing:

> When an individual is healed, s/he is 'at peace.' Healing also encompasses the idea of 'wholeness', which the Dinka value as a state of balanced and harmonious relationship between people, God, ancestors, and nature. Health is a state of complete well-being based on a way of living, conduct, and behaviour in relation to the others. It gives due respect to the dignity of the person and brings about a link of the person with God, ancestors, community, and environment.[2]

1. Bojuwoye, *Traditional Healing Practices*, 61.
2. Kamwaria and Michael, *The Role of African Tradition*, 52.

What the two Kenyatta University researchers found among the Dinka, holds very true to most of the African communities living in sub-Saharan Africa. Everything is connected, and for healing to be considered to have taken place there has to be a sense of homeostasis. The balance referred to above may not mean the total eradication of what initially caused the imbalance, but a consciousness, a sense of control and/or peace, is restored to the individual or community. As stated by the researchers above, healing has more of a relational aspect to it than just the eradication of a disease or illness. This is not to say that physical healing is not important to the African people, rather, in the processes of eliminating the ailment or illness, one has to consider the relational aspects of the healing activities. In terms of how most African communities view disease or illness, I would agree with Bujowoye who says that disease is not just a biological thing, but that it is associated with many aspects of the individual and/or community's life:

> The traditional African worldview also views disease not only as evidence of microbiological infection, but also as a breakdown in the physical, social and spiritual mechanisms of the individual and community. Disease is more a social construction, with the focus on the person-environment relationship, thus stressing the significance of interrelationship in healing. Disease is not just a physical fact but is associated with other aspects of life (including intellectual, emotional, social familial, occupational and spiritual dimensions . . . [3]

In other words, when a pandemic breaks out it throws everything out of balance, both the material and spiritual. Interpersonal relationships go out of sync. Kamwaria and Katola also found that among the traditional Dinka (African) community, the belief that illness or disease do not happen in isolation without other factors such as spiritual or sociological was and is still held true:

> Illness was perceived as a health disorder resulting from complex interaction of physical, spiritual, sociological, and physiological factors. In other words, illness was seen as psychosocial and psychosomatic. Restoration of health or healing was approached in terms of an interactive life process rather than just in terms of a bodily process. In this sense, healing acquired a broader dimension that included restoration of broken relationships between people and God, spirits, and environment. Healing was a holistic

---

3. Ibid., 63.

and transformative process of restoring troubled peace between people, God, spirits, and nature. It was a religious matter that had to be dealt with in a religious manner. The study noted that the Dinka health care system involves the whole community. Since healing is an interactive process, when one member of a community suffers from illness, everyone in the community suffers.[4]

Even in most modern day or contemporary Africa, this belief still exists. Healing is perceived in a holistic sense in the restorative or recovery processes. As stated earlier, homeostasis does not connote that everything goes back to the original state of affairs, but there has to be a sense of balance, a "new normal."

Another author, Mligo, writing on the same subject of healing in African contexts says the following:

> African Traditional religion, as with other world religions, is not a religion that has abandoned healing practices. Healing and wholeness is one of the sole concerns of this religion. . . . God's healing ministry cannot be localized only to what we call 'biomedicine,' and neither can we confine God's dealing with humanity to only one religion. If African Traditional Religion is a religion through which God's dealing with humanity is realized, then healing is among such dealings that God works in various ways to maintain wholeness among African people. . . . in the approach to healing of the whole person in the community (physically, mentally and spiritually) including the healing of relationships between people and their departed relatives and natural environment surrounding people, traditional healers are regarded as 'community workers' who serve the purposes of their community in various health matters.[5]

Mligo, in the above quotation, expands the understanding of healing to more than a physical cure. Healing has to involve both the seen and the unseen (the materialistic and the spiritual).

## A TWO-PRONG UNDERSTANDING TO HEALING

In this chapter, the word healing is used in reference to two different types of understandings that could be assumed in most sub-Sahara African contexts. The first is that healing means more that a cure, that is, "the

---

4. Ibid., 52.
5. Mligo, Shabani, and Elia, *Elements of African*, 52.

elimination or removal of a disease or its symptoms" as a definition.[6] In other words, the first premise of this author is that one can experience a cure without a sense of being healed. A person can be cured of an ailment, but psychologically, relationally, or spiritually continue to be haunted by the memories and/or struggle with one's perceptions to the event that caused the problem. A soldier who comes from a warfront may have his/her physical wounds cured, but carry much emotional and psychological woundedness (post-traumatic stress disorder–ptsd). The person may look physically healthy, but dying or dead psychologically, socially, and spiritually. At this level of understanding, healing would need to include a restoring of one's sense of meaning psychologically, relationally, spiritually, and the acceptance of one's physical condition in the recovery processes. This meaning would argue for a holistic understanding of healing.

A second understanding of healing is that which can also occur without a physical cure. When someone gets to a state of homeostasis in which one is totally at peace (psychologically, relationally and spiritually) with the circumstance s/he finds him/herself, even without attaining a physical cure to an ailment. This, the author believes, fits another definition of healing. In this sense, healing is not just the absence or presence of a disease, physical illness, or a disorder, but a sense of one's contentment, acceptance, and sense of meaning derived, despite one's physical condition. This should not also be mistaken with *denial*, which we know is a psychological/mental defense mechanism of one not accepting the external reality of that which one is dealing or facing. A person who has accepted his/her physical condition (even in a realistic face of death, without a physical cure), yet is totally at peace psychologically, relationally, and spiritually can be considered healed. Such a person has reached a state of homeostasis even without physically being cured.

My mother was born with perfect eyesight until the early 1990s when she had glaucoma, but was not initially diagnosed as such. The illness progressed without good treatment, with her eye doctor mostly to blame for her situation. When, I went back to Zimbabwe in 1997 for research, I took my mother to another eye doctor who became angry with me for not having taken my mother to an optometrist or ophthalmologists earlier. He mentioned that if the illness had been attended to 5 years earlier, her eyesight would have been saved. I explained that I had, but that the previous doctor said the medicine he had prescribed was all he could give even

---

6. The New Oxford American Dictionary, (Online).

though it had not helped. This was said in the presence of my mother and all she could say was, "he tried." Surgery was done, however, after about two months my mother became completely blind. My dad became my mother's eyes and in 2003 he passed away, leaving her without much freedom.

On one of my trips back to Zimbabwe in 2010, my mother took me aside. She said, *"Son, I have something I have always wanted to tell you. I want to thank you for all the effort you put in trying to have me re-gain my sight. I know what the second doctor said to you might have hurt you because you had tried, but I did not defend you enough."* She went on to say, *"When you had taken me to the second doctor I already had accepted that I was not going to receive my sight back because the Lord had already revealed this to me in a dream."* She agreed to go through with the visit and the surgery, since God works in mysterious ways. My mother said, *"that even though she had not received her physical eyesight, she now had a set of "new eyes."* She told me that she now could see things that she had never been able to see with her physical eyes. One of the blessings she said she now had received, was that she was no longer able to judge people based on their looks (light or dark skinned, clothes they wear, ugly, or such,), only those with physical eyes struggle with that kind of judgment. Through her set of "new eyes," she now was able to "see" everyone as a child of God. This, she said, she had received as a gift and it gave her peace, and now she took her blindness as a blessing rather than a curse. She said, *"When I started loosing my sight, I yearned for "a cure" to my eyesight and was angry with God. However, through my journey, the loosing of my sight helped me to receive "complete healing," especially in many areas of my life I had neglected, which was judging others based on their looks."* The journey with her blindness helped her to be "totally healed," emotionally, relationally, and spiritually in her relations to others and God.

My mother is not a "saint," but she is one of the most spiritual people I know who taught me this lesson about healing in life, which I would have missed. She received healing without a cure for her eyesight.

It is these two worldviews to healing: (a) a holistic, and (b) healing that may not result in a physical cure, however, with one experiencing "a peace of God which surpasses all understanding"[7] –relationally, psychologically, and spiritually that this author believes can be found in some communities in Sub-Saharan Africa. It is this author's argument that there are some people living or dying of HIV & AIDS, but have acquired a sense of peace

---

7. Philippians 4:7, ESV.

relationally, psychologically, and spiritually without attaining a physical cure. Provided the right and accepting environments, and symbolic rituals, it can be argued, that these individuals would experience healing without the physical cure. Their physical abilities/disabilities or the diseases that they carry are no longer what is used to judge or measure their "humanness." It is by creating loving environments were rituals of forgiveness, reconciliation, and offering them a sense of dying in and with dignity that is an ultimate healing that they be accorded.

This author realizes, and is well aware, that Africa is a continent and that healing practices and beliefs are not homogeneous. There are, however, certain traditional practices and beliefs that form a "homophonic rhythm" and are knitted into the fabric of most African people's worldview. The beliefs and worldview about healing represents one of those common fundamentals found in most of these communities. What one would find are variations to these practices and beliefs, however, there are within them foundational similarities in core values. One of the questions this chapter will wrestle with is how, in general, healing is perceived in many of the African contexts, especially in the face of illnesses such as HIV/AIDS. These two diseases are especially known to have no known cures. Science has not given us any answers to the total eradication of these deadly diseases. Given the fact that these diseases are going to be with these communities for years to come, does it mean that the communities or individuals affected can never achieve a sense of healing? Does it mean that these individuals/communities will live in perpetual brokenness or fractured sense of wholeness? In other words, what does healing look like in the face of these diseases or illness? Can healing be experienced without a cure being found?

Graham acknowledges the need for the Western approaches to pay attention to the indigenous understandings of healing. He says:

> Another frontier is the need to develop models of healing which bring social, political, economic, and ecological dimensions of health and healing into the dialogue with spiritual, emotional, and physical. Neither the Charismatic-sacramental nor the pastoral-psychotherapeutic approaches have transcended their foundations in individual psychology and Western bourgeois culture. In addition, there is need for pastoral theological interpretations of healing to incorporate perspectives and practices from Native American, Asian, African, and Spiritualistic sources. Rather than being seen as superstitious and primitive, these powerful orientations may enable us to further regain wholism of our early Judaic

and Christian heritage and to more fully witness to the saving power of God in the world.[8]

I echo Graham's argument and sentiments in the above paragraph in that many times the indigenous perspectives to a vast majority of issues, especially health and spirituality, were and continue to be overshadowed by the Western approaches. The indigenous people's methods have been looked upon as backward, unscientific, and primitive.[9] Interestingly, it is these "indigenous knowledges" that served these contexts before the advent of colonization and Christianity. It is high time we integrate these traditional proven practices with today's scientific discoveries rather than throwing out the "baby and the bath water."

## HEALING: SYMBOLIC ACTS, RITUALS, AND RELATIONSHIPS

In traditional and today's African worldview about healing, ritual practices, symbols, and the processes of the righting of relationships are foundational and central to the outcome. Dube says about the centrality of rituals and relationships in healing processes,

> "sometimes reconciliation rituals may be needed. . . . Unhealthy relationships, in other words are held to be integral part of one's ill-health. . . . Physical healing of the body is thus accompanied by healing of relationships. Consequently, healing is regarded as healing of all relationships. Health is, therefore, closely tied to healthy relationships and ill-health closely tied to unhealthy relationships. This philosophy requires an ethic of being responsible for one's own health and for that of others through maintaining healthy relationships. The healing of relationships is integral to healing of pain."[10]

The important point being made in the above paragraph is that "good health" is not limited to good physical health. There is a connection to the physical, social, and spiritual when life goes out of balance. The idea of ill-health also involves the unseen and/or spiritual matters. The idea of healing and health being holistic is shared by some in the Western world as well, especially those who have a religious bent to the way they live their life.

---

8. Graham, *Healing*, 501.
9. Mucherera, *Meet me at the Palaver*, 7.
10. Ibid., 143.

There are those who also believe, from a Christian perspective, that healing encompasses spirituality and relationships as well.

Healing is the process of being restored to bodily wholeness, emotional well-being, mental functioning, and spiritual aliveness. Christian modes of healing have always distinguished themselves by achieving a spiritual advance in connection with the healing process. Healing may also refer to the process of reconciling of broken healing relationships and to the development of a social and political order among races and nations . . . there is a social dimension to salvation and health, which attends it, extending to relationships among nations as well as an ecological dimensions involving stewardship of the earth. Thus, healing and salvation are linked insofar as they both involve restoration to dynamic wholeness in body, mind, spirit, society and the world, and derive from being in proper relation to God.[11]

The above understanding of healing is similar to what prevails in most of the African contexts south of the Sahara. Healing is beyond just the physical aspect but encompasses relationships and one spiritual dimension. Bojuwoye, quoting Ngubane, says the following about disease/illness and good health:

> Africans recognize some illnesses as natural ones that "just happen," particularly illnesses such as influenza, measles, chicken pox, diarrhea, fever, headache, and others that are seen as requiring simple treatment by home remedies. . . . the most satisfactory form of explanation is that which explains the purpose of an event and also identifies the force behind it, and these are the steps in the process employed to diagnose diseases, plan treatment strategies, and promote good health.[12]

The point is that besides using the herbs or medicines to treat diseases, there are, in most African contexts, rituals that should be performed in the processes of healing. Once in a while, even those illnesses that are presumed natural when they become a pandemic, the community is called upon to do and/or perform certain rituals as way to combat the epidemic. Bojuwore further says:

> The negative forces undermining human integrity, making people ill, or destroying people's lives may indeed be parts of the essence of life that people have to live with through processes of negotiation and accommodation. Hence, African traditional healing is

11. . Graham, *Healing*, 497.
12. Bojuwoye, *Traditional Healing Practices*, 64.

> not just for symptom removal or exorcism. Apart from prescription of herbs (or medicines) to deal with physical symptoms of diseases, traditional healers also prescribe rituals to restore harmony, especially between people. . . . Rituals are symbolic group activities or procedures prepared in a natural way in societies and families to guide and facilitate social and individual change. Rituals are culturally organized, symbolically meaningful activities that provide standardized therapeutic experiences for reduction of anxiety and emotional distress. A ritual ceremony brings people and all elements (living and nonliving) of the universe together. Rituals unite people together and are avenues for mediating relationship behaviors to influence the way individuals and families treat each other.[13]

What is stated in the paragraph above shows the importance of symbolic activities that accompany the healing processes. In traditional and/ or most of modern day Africa, it is not a matter of getting the herbs or prescribed medicines, but that there are symbolic activities that are tied to the key processes of healing. The rituals involved have a psychological, social, and relational purpose.

Growing up we used to laugh at my father after returning from visiting our family medical doctor. Whenever he went for a medical visit and after the doctor examined him, then offered him "just pills" without an injection, he would say that the doctor did not treat him "very well" since he did not get an injection. For my father, psychologically the ritual of being given an injection was key to his treatment processes. Not everyone agreed with my father, since when my younger brother and I visited a doctor for treatment, we felt better if we were offered pills without an injection. As for my brother and I, what was important was the ritual of touch. If the doctor did not examine and/or touch us, but just talked and asked questions, in our minds the ritual was not as complete. In short, the ritual of touch or interaction with the medicine person (doctor) and taking home some form of medicine was psychologically very important to us. In both instances, there were variations in how we viewed the rituals with the doctor. However, for our family doctor, his goal in working with us was to achieve good health. The point being that, as much as the ritual practices may differ from one African context to another, the goal to heal is the same. Variations in practices are common, however, it is important to note the centrality of rituals, even in the modern day African Christian communities. What rituals do is that

13. Ibid., 64.

they bring or draw people together. One cannot not relate once in the midst of others. In other words, once present at the ritual, somehow one is forced to find a way to participate, and relationships are forged or formed. Those relationships that need to be repaired are attended to in the midst of others.

Having served in churches in Zimbabwe as a pastor, there are certain ritual practices expected by the parishioners. If they come to share their problems with their pastor, they also expect a prayer from the pastor. In these African contexts, pastors do not counsel or provide pastoral care with a parishioner or family and then send the person(s) away at the end of the session without praying for the person(s). Even when conducting pastoral visits in homes, at the end of the visit a pastor is expected to offer a word of prayer. Some may even ask to be prayed over by laying-on of hands. Parishioners in most denominations, including mainline churches, expect this ritual of prayer from their pastors. In indigenous Christian churches (Utopia, Zion Apostolic, Independent churches, Johanne Marange and Masowe, now common in many countries in sub-Sahara African), the parishioner may have oil smeared over their forehead or body, or water poured or sprinkled over them. Some are given the oil or 'holy water' to take home to mix with their bath water, and continue using as a symbol of cleansing and combating any evil attacks. Others are given small stones, ashes, or leaves, etc., to place in their drinking water for internal cleansing and to rid of the ailments. In mainline denominations where the members wear church uniforms, some pastors will pray for the uniform belt, hat, or dress and the person will have these in their home when needed. The symbols of water, oil, cloth, a Bible, leaves, ashes, or stones have become incorporated in the rituals of healing. Any water, oil, cloth, or symbols prayed over by the pastor are no longer ordinary but "holy elements." These holy elements are used as protection symbols to the spiritual or physical attacks one could experience after leaving the prayer service or in the absence of the pastor. This belief is very much similar to what we see with the Apostle Paul in the book of Acts 19: "God was performing extraordinary miracles by the hands of Paul, so that handkerchiefs or aprons were even carried from his body to the sick and the diseases left them and the evil spirits went out."[14]

There is a sense in which many people psychologically want something tangible to take home. The laying on of hands and the imposition of oil has become a common practice even in some of the mainline denominations. These ritual practices of healing were common in the African

---

14. Acts 19:11–12, SV.

traditional worldview and are still present in today's contemporary African Christian context.

## CHRIST'S HEALING MINISTRY

## A Synopsis

There are common aspects of the African worldview about healing that are very similar to the Judeo-Christian practices, (rituals of cleansing) and also as seen in the life and ministry of Christ. In this section of the chapter, we will focus on the healing ministry of Jesus Christ and how it illustrates and mirrors some of the healing practices or rituals as practiced in traditional Africa and in the contemporary context today. The specific stories used to illustrate these similarities are: the crippled man at the pool (John 5:1–17; the story of the man born blind (John 9); the ten lepers (Luke 17:11–19); the Samaritan woman at the well (John 4ff); and the woman caught in adultery (John 8:1ff).

## The Crippled Man at the Pool

Below is part of the first story of the crippled man at the pool (John 5:1–17):

> After this there was a feast of the Jews, and Jesus went up to Jerusalem. Now there is in Jerusalem by the Sheep Gate a pool, in Aramaic called Bethesda, which has five roofed colonnades. In these lay a multitude of invalids—blind, lame, and paralyzed. *(for an angel of the Lord went down at certain seasons into the pool, and stirred up water; whoever stepped in first after the stir of the water was made well from whatever disease the person had).* One man was there who had been an invalid for thirty-eight years. When Jesus saw him lying there and knew that he had already been there a long time, he said to him, "Do you want to be healed?" The sick man answered him, "Sir, I have no one to put me into the pool when the water is stirred up, and while I am going another steps down before me." Jesus said to him, "Get up, take up your bed, and walk." 9 And at once the man was healed, and he took up his bed and walked. . . . Now the man who had been healed did not know who it was, for Jesus had withdrawn, as there was a crowd in the place. Afterward Jesus found him in the temple and said to him, "See, you are well! Sin no more, that nothing worse may

happen to you." The man went away and told the Jews that it was Jesus who had healed him.[15]

The story above initially presents the cultural worldview of the Jewish community about the cleansing activities at the pool of Bethesda. "Bethesda" is Aramaic and it means "House of Mercy."[16] Annually, the angel of the Lord would come and stir the waters of the pool, and whoever was first to jump into the pool was cleansed of their infirmities (leprosy, blindness, etc.,). Water represented cleansing, so whoever went into the pool was cured of his or her ailment. The angel stirring the waters of the pool and the first person jumping in, was the sequence to this healing ritual.

The second part of the story indicated that after Jesus cured the man, he (the man) walked away. Jesus does not use the word "healed" in talking to the man, but it is the writer of John who says, "now that the man had been healed." The author of John equates the physical cure with healing, as is common usage of the word. It is interesting that when Jesus meets the man in the temple for the second time he says, "See, you are well! Sin no more, that nothing worse may happen to you" (John 5:14).

The Jewish tradition believed that for someone to be born crippled, his or her parents or the person had to have sinned.[17] Jesus' words echoed the "common knowledge" or the traditional understanding familiar to the man that sin is what had put him in his predicament. However, Jesus healing ministry in general is a challenge to this belief, and his words are a call to this formerly crippled man to live a righteous, upright and holy life (socially, physically, spiritually and mentally). In tracing the meaning of healing, Graham states that the New Testament times always perceived healing holistically.

> The New Testament regards healing as an indication of the presence of the Kingdom of God in which restoration of the bodily wholeness, emotional well-being, and mental functioning take place in the context of a spiritual advance. . . . Illness and disease were regarded as forms of bondage to evil forces, taking place in the depths of personal being apart from personal choice or control.

---

15. John 5:1–17, ESV.

16. Easton Bible Dictionary, http://www.biblestudytools.com/dictionary/bethesda/, house of mercy, a reservoir (Gr. kolumbethra, "a swimming bath") with five porches, close to the sheep-gate or market (Nehemiah 3:1 ; John 5:2 ). Eusebius the historian (A.D. 330) calls it "the sheep-pool."

17. John 9:1ff, ESV.

Jesus' method of healing evoked latent attitudes of faith and the desire for wholeness and linked these with the healing power of God who hates evil in all in its forms. Restoration of bodily, emotional, and mental capacities were not the only concern of this new order, but restoration of these faculties was included in it.[18]

When Jesus met the man at the pool, he offered him what he had wanted for the 38-years he had stayed by the pool–physical cure. However, when Jesus met the man in the temple, he received complete restoration–Jesus made him well. The "wellness" Jesus pronounced to this man in the temple is beyond "physical wellness," since he told the man to "sin" more." When Jesus said that, the man was now "well," there was a spiritual aspect added to the healing. There was no need for Jesus to pronounce that the man had been made well, and for him not to sin anymore, if the man had been totally healed at the pool. When the man met Jesus at the pool, he received a physical cure to his ailment *and* a social restoration to his position in society. He could now cross the barriers of social isolation, and was now able to enter the temple. However, the completeness to his healing occurred in the temple after Christ pronounced that the man's faith had made him "well." It is interesting to note that it is only after he receives his spiritual healing that the man recognizes Jesus. The relational aspects of this story is very important, he is now socially acceptable and no longer a social and spiritual outcast of the society. The event is public, there are witnesses to the healing, and relationships are restored.

Healing in the African context includes reconciliation, and bringing human relationships back into balance. It goes beyond the individual self-interests of health (from the "I" to "we") to one realizing one's health depends on that of others. I agree with Pobee, an African theologian, about what he sees as the difference between the Western and African human existence:

> "Whereas Descartes spoke for Western man when he said *cogito ergo sum*–I think, therefore I exist–Akan (African) man's (sic) ontology is *cognatus ergo sum*–I am related by blood, therefore I exist, or I exist because I belong to a family. . . . the family relationships determine the view of man."[19]

---

18. Graham, *Healing*, 498.
19. Pobee, John. *Toward an African Theology*. 49.

The implications of the story of the crippled man being healed by Jesus, illustrates that Jesus restored both the sense of "I am" (individuality) and "we are" (a sense of communal belonging), in the man.[20]

In yet another story, Christ's healing ministry proves a holistic understanding-physical, social, and spiritual, and includes some forms of a ritual. This is the story of a man blind from birth who received his sight after meeting Christ and his disciples:

> When he had said this, he spat on the ground and made mud with the saliva and spread the mud on the man's eyes, saying to him, "Go wash in the pool of Siloam" (which means Sent). Then he went and washed and came back able to see. The neighbors and those who had seen him before as a beggar began to ask, "Is this not the man who used to sit and beg?" Some were saying, "It is he." Others were saying, "No but it is someone like him." He kept saying, "I am the man". . . . Jesus heard that they had driven him out and when he found him he said, "Do you believe in the Son of Man?" He answered, "And who is he, sir?" Tell me, so that I may believe in him." Jesus said to him, "You have seen him, and the one speaking with you is he." He said, "Lord I believe." And he worshipped him. Jesus said, I came into this world for judgment so that those who do not see may see, and those who do see may become blind."[21]

Part of the symbolic ritual that Christ performs in the story above is the process of cleansing. The mud and saliva symbolize the cleansing activity. To complete the cleansing process Christ asks the man to go wash at the pool of Siloam. Again water, which was and is still used in cleansing ceremonies, takes its central place.

The man was still blind when he was told to go wash at the pool, meaning someone had to walk him there. Those who used to walk him to the place he usually sat to beg, now have to walk with him to the pool of Siloam. Indirectly, Jesus' action with this blind man is an invitation to others to participate in the journey of this man's healing. Even though not directly mentioned in the text, it can be insinuated that family members or some from the community were somehow involved as well in this man's journey to and the symbolic ritual of cleansing at the pool.

Jesus could have just opened the eyes of this man privately, (whom the community considered an outcast and sinner), but he chose this to

20. John 5:1–17, NRSV.
21. NRSV

be a public event. In the text it is pointed out that after the man received his sight some believed it was the man, and others said he was not. From among those who said he was, it could be intimated they had followed the blind man and were witnesses to his being able to see again after he washed his eyes.

The next time Jesus meets the man, the conversation moves from the man being cured of his physical blindness to spiritual sightedness. The first question Jesus asked the man is whether he believed in the Son of Man, the Messiah. Then man asked who the Son of man was and Jesus says he was. When Jesus responded by, "you have seen him," He is no longer talking about physical sightedness, but spiritual, so much so that the Pharisees reacted negatively to Jesus. The man had not just been healed from physical blindness, but that he could now see spiritually as well. He was now set free from being a social outcast and from traditionally being perceived as born in sin. If he had not met Jesus for the second time, this man would have been cured of his physical blindness, but would not have attained the spiritual freedom in Christ. Again, this story illustrates Jesus's healing ministry as holistic.

The theme of setting people (social outcasts) free, physically and spiritually, is consistent in Jesus ministry. The community, rituals, restoration of relationships, and spiritual freedom are aspects of healing that is part of the traditional African worldview and practices today. Ritual practices have been passed from generation to generation, even though with variations due to the fact that culture is not static but dynamic. Freedman and Combs, (even though writing from a Western point of view), echo the realities of today's modern African worldview pertaining to the importance of rituals, customs, and social realities.

> the beliefs, values, institutions, customs, labels, laws, divisions of labor, and the like that make up our social realities are constructed by the members of a culture as they interact with one another from generation to generation and day to day. That is, societies construct the "lenses" through which their members interpret the world. The realities that each of us takes for granted are the realities that our societies have surrounded us with since birth. These realities provide the beliefs, practices, words, and experiences from which we make up our lives, or as we would say in postmodernist jargon, "constitute our selves."[22]

---

22. Freedman and Combs, *Narrative Therapy*, 16.

Beliefs and ritual practices passed on from previous generations form the lenses through which today's African communities need to understand the ideas of healing. As stated earlier, these beliefs have been inherited and will be passed on to the next generation.

Another story illustrating Jesus' healing ministry is when he cured or cleansed ten lepers. This is another one of those stories that demonstrates Jesus' holistic approach to healing.

> On the way to Jerusalem he was passing along between Samaria and Galilee. And as he entered a village, he was met by ten lepers, who stood at a distance and lifted up their voices, saying, "Jesus, Master, have mercy on us." When he saw them he said to them, "Go and show yourselves to the priests." And as they went they were cleansed. Then one of them, when he saw that he was healed, turned back, praising God with a loud voice; and he fell on his face at Jesus' feet, giving him thanks. Now he was a Samaritan. Then Jesus answered, "Were not ten cleansed? Where are the nine? Was no one found to return and give praise to God except this foreigner?" And he said to him, "Rise and go your way; your faith has made you well."[23]

The Jewish tradition was such that if someone was infected or thought they had the leprosy disease, they would go to a priest, who would observe the person for seven days.[24] After the seven-day period, the priest would declare the person clean or unclean. Inline with the tradition, Jesus tells the lepers to go show themselves to the priests so as to be observed and/or for the priest to perform the traditional rituals for them to be declared clean. In the text (the EVS version), it is interesting that the translation does not use the word 'healed,' but that as they were on their way the lepers were "cleansed." There were ten lepers, nine being Jews (given Christ's response in the passage) and the one who returned being a Samaritan. Since he was a Samaritan he probably knew he could not enter the temple to show himself to the priest. The author of Luke seem to emphasize the idea that it was through pure gratitude that the leper came back to Jesus as soon as he realized he was now clean. Jesus pronounced to the man that it was through his "faith" that he had been made "well." Again, Jesus uses the word "well" not "cleansed." In meeting with Christ for the second time, the leper is more than physically cleansed, he is made "wholly well," in other words, healed.

23. Luke 17:11–19, ESV.
24. Leviticus 13:1ff, ESV.

It can be argued that the nine lepers were cleansed–they got a "cure," and the one who came back received total "healing." When Jesus said that it was the man's faith that made him well, it is implied that whatever brought the man back to Jesus, the others did not receive or lacked. The man came to thank God and worshipped Christ, for he "fell on his face at Jesus' feet and thanked him. It can be assumed that "the faith that made him well," applied to more than the physical condition, to include his spiritual condition.

In this story we again see a restoration of relationships (social), health (physical), and spiritual. The point being that healing usually includes these three aspects not just physical, a worldview that is inline with the African perception. In the above stories the starting point for the individual's healing was physical but the process eventually encompassed other aspects of the person's life. The next two stories are used to illustrate how Jesus healed (spiritually, socially, and physically) two different women even though their point of contact with Christ was relational; they needed to be freed (spiritually). In the end, the women experienced complete healing–spiritually, socially, and physically, as well.

## Jesus and the Samaritan Woman at the Well

A starting point of the encounter between Jesus and the Samaritan woman (John 4:7ff) at the well, is the need for spiritual and relational healing—she is living in sin. The woman was a social outcast who had lived with five men (and probably abused by these men) and the sixth man with whom she was currently living was not her husband. It is sin that was binding her to these unhealthy "social relations, " and she was spiritually lost. When Jesus asked her for a drink, (she wondered why a Jew would ask of a drink from a Samaritan), Jesus moved the conversation from material things to a spiritual level. He responded: "If you knew the gift of God, and who it is that is saying to you, 'Give me a drink,' you would have asked him and he would have given you living water."[25] The conversation continues until the woman realizes that Jesus is the Messiah. After meeting Christ, she is "completely *spiritually* and *psychologically* alive" and she *physically* went back into the community to share about her life-changing encounter with Christ, which then led others to spiritual salvation. The highlight of the story is that the event is so public that everyone in the community heard about the woman's encounter and experience with Christ.

25. John 4ff, NRSV.

> "Many Samaritans from the city believed in him (Jesus) because of the woman's testimony. He told me everything I have ever done.... They said to the woman, 'It is no longer because of what you said that we believe, for we have heard for ourselves, and know that this is truly the Savior of the world.'"[26]

Having encountered Christ, the woman not only experienced psychological and social freedom, but spiritual healing. As a "new creation," with salvation in her wings, it gave her the courage to go back to a community that used to despise her. The community's response to this public healing was that of celebration of the woman's testimony. Her healing also led to the community's healing. This is the way healing must be perceived in modern day Africa if we are to succeed in the war against the HIV & AIDS pandemic. Holistic healing has to bring transformation not only to the individual but to the community as well. Attitudes and responses to the woman in the story were changed, relationships were restored, forgiveness, and reconciliation were achieved.

## Jesus and the Woman Caught in Adultery

In the story of the woman caught in adultery,[27] about to be stoned to death, (not only does Jesus save her from a physical death sentence, but also frees her from spiritual death).

> The scribes and Pharisees brought a woman who had been caught in adultery; and making her stand before all of them, they said to him, "Teacher, this woman was caught in the very act of committing adultery. Now in the law Moses commanded us to stone such women. Now what do you say?" . . . Jesus bent down and wrote with his finger on the ground." When they kept questioning him, he straightened up and said to them, "Let anyone among you who is without sin be the first to throw a stone at her." . . . When they heard this they went away one by one beginning with the elders; and Jesus was left alone with the woman standing before him. Jesus straightened up and said to her, "Woman, where are they? Has no one condemned you?" She said, "No one sir," and Jesus said, "Neither do I condemn you. Go your way, and from now on do not sin again."

26. Ibid.
27. John 8:1ff, NRSV.

The starting point of change for the woman is in how Jesus responded to the Pharisees, indicating their need for transformation as well as that of the woman's spiritual life. She had been living in sin and was caught in the very act of adultery. Her spiritual salvation leads her to being freed in the society. She is no longer a social outcast (relationally), mentally, and emotionally based on her previous life, having received healing from Christ. The healing gives her the courage to face those who had used, or abused, and viewed her as none other than a sexual object. The healing is a public event and she goes back publicly to share her new found freedom spiritually, socially, and psychologically.

In all the different stories used above illustrating Jesus healing ministry, everything was done in public, not in private. Even the Samaritan woman (John 4ff) who met Jesus privately at the well (with the disciples arriving later at the scene), having believed in Jesus, went back to share with others the good news about Christ. She made her encounter with Christ public by making it known to the community. The same is true of the woman caught in adultery (John 8ff), Jesus tells her to go back to the community and to sin no more.

The healing practices of Christ were mostly public events. People were healed in front of crowds or in places where there were witnesses to the healings. In many instances, Christ also told people to go back to their families/homes to go tell what the Lord had done for them, etc., and/or to show themselves to the priests. Healing was not a private matter, as it was a public event that needed to be celebrated and witnessed by the community.

## HEALING IN THE AGE OF HIV & AIDS

As posited earlier, illnesses and/or diseases in most African context are not just limited to a matter of physical infection or pain. Beyond the question of how the illness came about, is the question of why the illness, and what needs to take place for healing to occur. The illness of HIV/AIDS in Africa, usually treated using Western medicine, have raised the question about "healing" given that illnesses and diseases are perceived very differently in most African contexts. The treatments for such illnesses have been privatized in the West, quite the opposite of communally oriented African contexts.

HIV & AIDS brings the relationship of the rights of the individual and the community into critical focus. That is, what does it mean to be faithful to the ethic "I am because we are, and we are because I am," an ethic that must takes both the individual and the community seriously? Given the socially driven face of HIV & AIDS, an exclusive focus on the individual's physical symptoms and treatment as a private secret of the infected and the affected aided the spread of the pandemic itself rather than prevention. Such an approach has not even protected the individual, let alone the community.[28] I agree with Dube that healing is not a private matter since the African contexts are communally oriented. The community is actively involved in the healing processes of those fallen to the infection. The following discussion is about confidentiality; health and healing in communally oriented communities such as sub-Saharan Africa.

## HEALING AS A PUBLIC EVENT, VERSUS CONFIDENTIALITY IN AFRICA

The traditional African healing practices were not normally a private affair. If someone became sick it was the immediate/extended families and/or community's role to help find a cure. The issue was never just between the medicine person and the patient. The current *confidentiality policies* tied to the issues of HIV/AIDS are a borrowed practice from the West. This is not to say there is no confidentiality in the African context, but that the Western rules guiding the practice were never contextualized to protect both the individual and the community. The Western world is after the protection and autonomy of the individual while the African context starts with the protection of the community at the same time respecting the rights of the individual. The rules and guidelines of confidentiality enforced today in African contexts in treating HIV/AIDS follow HIPAA laws, which are all Western by design:

> The individual who is the subject of the protected health information can exercise all rights granted by the HIPAA Privacy Rule with respect to all protected health information about him or her, including information obtained while the individual was an unemancipated minor consistent with State or other law. Generally, the parent would no longer be the personal representative of his or her child once the child reaches the age of majority or becomes

---

28. Dube, *Adikira*, 139.

emancipated, and therefore, would no longer control the health information about his or her child."[29]

It is also interesting that in most African countries, following the Western standards, the majority age is now generally 18 years of age. How does one just transplant a rule from one context to another without honoring the worldview, practices, and beliefs of those affected and/or infected? The meaning of healing in the Western world involves protection of the individual right and autonomy. In the West, information about an illness is between the doctor and the patient. Even when the parents are paying the bills of their child (18years of age), they cannot obtain the records of their child's illness without the child's consent. Someone could secretly, (between the patient and doctor), live with an illness without family members knowing how to help. These policies of autonomy have become the practice in African societies as it pertains to HIV/AIDS, and many people are dying lonely while protecting their illness at the expense of their relationships. Dube says the following about the impact of the introduction of the confidentiality policy on the continent especially in relationship to HIV/AIDS:

> The policy of confidentiality spun a virtual shroud of secrecy, shame, and fear around the pandemic as something that should not be openly shared. It sent a message that seemingly said, 'HIV & AIDS are not diseases like all other diseases that we have had to tackle together; rather, they are the burden of the individuals.' . . . Among the infected who found themselves called to carry their crosses alone, the policy of confidentiality groomed anger, leading at times to the deliberate infection of others. . . . the confidentiality policy raised fear, shame, isolation, rejection, anger, stigma, and discrimination to even greater levels . . . Not only did individuals fear that some people –family, spouses, friends, workmates, church members or their own children—would find out about their status, but also became afraid of finding out for and about themselves. Keeping such a big secret is, in itself, an incredible burden of ill-health.[30]

The introduction of confidentiality, packaged together with HIV & AIDS in many sub-Saharan Africa or indigenous contexts, stigmatized the illnesses. The issue of confidentiality has made many people in African communities experience lonely deaths. It never used to be that people

29. Hippa.
30. Dube, *Adikira*, 138.

would choose to die lonely, since, traditionally; illnesses were viewed as the family's burden, not a secret between the patient and the doctor. In many cases, if the person visited the medicine person's home seeking a cure, family members would camp or live with the medicine person's family for a time. The family was involved fully in the treatment of the ill person. There was no confidentiality among family members, patient, and the medicine person as to the illness. In other words, the healing process involved members of the family. Illnesses such as HIV/AIDS became shameful to disclose because of stigmatization, thus, people started cutting themselves off emotional, spiritually, relationally, and then dying isolated. In general, pandemic illnesses used to be public information for the family so as to find help, but now it has become privatized, and it is killing people physically as well as mentally, spiritually, and relationally. People are dying alone, and lonely deaths have always been perceived as one of the worst things to ever happen to a person. Confidentiality (the way of HIPAA), in the traditional context, has become "a silent secret killer," since its not holistic in nature nor in its approach.

Dr. Chimedza, a medical practitioner in Zimbabwe, raised this concern in a column that he contributed through a local state-run newspaper. This citation has been used in another writing[31] and it is worthwhile to cite most of Dr. Chimedza's article here as an example of the magnitude of the HIV/AIDS problem and the issue of confidentiality. He writes:

> Sometime in 1999 I was looking after a certain couple living positively with HIV and AIDS. The wife then passed away. Six months down the line the husband (50 years old) brought a 17-year-old girl to me and introduced her as his new wife. Naturally I was very worried that the 17-year-old was going to be infected so I secretly raised my concern with the patient and implored on him to inform his new wife about his HIV status. He said, "Chiremba don't worry, I will strictly and consistently use condoms with her and *inini ndakura munyaya dzebode, ndava kungoda kuti agozondichengetawo.* I am not really very crazy about sex anymore. I am just looking for someone to take care of me." He promised to tell her about his status but he never got around to doing it. On putting more pressure on him to disclose his status to the wife, he changed doctors. Eight months down the line he came back because his wife was now pregnant and he wanted me to institute measures to prevent infection of the baby by the HIV virus. On doing the HIV test the

---

31. Mucherera, *Meet me at the Palaver*, 43–44.

wife was also now positive. I felt terrible that she had been infected while I looked on. Medical ethics and confidentiality prevented me from informing the young girl that her husband was living positively with HIV and AIDS. She never got the opportunity to take adequate precautions to prevent infection from her husband because she didn't know. . . . Why is it that with HIV and AIDS we get so passionate about confidentiality and human rights that we watch people getting infected and do nothing about it? What about the rights of those being infected? I am sure 80 percent of Zimbabweans who are negative have a right to be protected from the infection and the 20 percent who are positive also have a right to be protected from re-infecting. . . . [32]

The point Dr. Chimedza is making above in dealing with health issues, is of utter importance understanding the values, worldviews, and practices of the communities the intervention is taking place. It is easy for the developed and scientific world to enter an environment with "ready made solutions," without consulting the ones receiving the help on how to contextualize the intervention, since in most cases "the beggar is not the chooser."

## IMPLICATIONS CHRIST'S HEALING MINISTRY TO THE MODERN AFRICAN CONTEXT

The traditional African worldview, and some aspects of the ministry of Christ's healing ministry explored above, have implications on how healing ministries could be practiced in contemporary sub-Saharan Africa. A few of the components that this author believes are relevant points raised in this chapter that need to be considered in the healing ministries on the continent, and in fighting against the HIV & AIDS pandemic: a.) re-villaging as key to healing, b.) healing as relational and communal event, c.) healing using palaver rituals, d.) religious leaders take a central role in the healing ministry, but refrain from abuse of their position.

---

32. Chimedza, *Let's do SARS*. Dr P. Chimedza is a medical practitioner with a special interest in HIV and Aids. Information for this article was researched from different medical textbooks, medical journals and other medical information sources for which this author hereby acknowledges. This column is kindly sponsored by Generation Health. For further information on this topic and suggestions on future topics for discussion you can mail him on pchimedza@hotmail.com

## RE-VILLAGING AS KEY TO HEALING

The sub-Sahara African context today needs a blending of the past "indigenous knowledges" and the present Christian understandings to combat the HIV/AIDS pandemic. The healing ministry of the church could be aided by reclaiming some of the re-villaging concepts. Re-villaging is the reclaiming of some of the core values from traditional African practices. The village provided the cultural and religious foundations for the individuals and their communities. The individual got his or her psychological, mental, physical, and spiritual support, upbringing, and identity from the village. I agree with Wimberly and Mucherera in how they perceive the functions of the village, and how these could be integrated in today's context of the church's healing ministry.

> Re-villaging refers to the attempt . . . to re-establish selective village functions such as symbolizing, support/maintenance, ritualizing, and mentoring. . . . a) Symbolizing function is the organizing of the life of the village around a particular story and sub-stories that provide an overarching system that gives meaning to every aspect of life; b) Support/maintenance function provides cross-generational relational ties for people that help them maintain emotional, physical, and spiritual well being in the face of life transitions and difficulty; c) Mentoring function refers to providing the next generation opportunities to be integrated into the community's meaning system through their internalization of attitudes, scenes, roles, and story plots; d) Ritualizing function provides repetitive patterns for re-enforcing symbolizing, support/maintenance, and mentoring functions.[33]

Today, the church is strategically positioned to take the role of re-villaging, especially in the face of this pandemic. It is the role of the pastors and congregants to support those families that are infected and affected instead of ostracizing them. In addition, if mentoring of the youth and young adults takes a priority, this allows for the church to be influential before they (youth and young adults) find themselves infected. The symbolizing functions of church is to educate the youth and young adults on questions such as: "What does it mean to say I am a man and what are the Christian moral guides as it pertains to manhood?" "How do I treat women in my life

---

33. Wimberly and Mucherera presented the idea of re-villaging in an unpublished paper at the Forth (4th) Congress of the African Association of Pastoral Studies and Counseling in Yaounde Cameroon, July 27, 2001.

as a Christian young man, despite what my peers, culture, and the media may say?" To the girls and young women, the church symbolizing function is that of training about self-respect, peer pressure, and not buying into the popular culture of looking at the self as a sexual object. Young girls are to be encouraged to see themselves and view their bodies as being formed and created in the image of God. The purpose of God creating women was/is not to just provide sexual pleasure to man, but rather to be a companion. The supporting and maintenance is that of accountability, role modeling, and creating mentoring groups for the youth and young adults early in life. Most of the role models the youth and young adults see through media are not realistic, in that many are "Hollywood" creations.

Rituals, relationships and openness, were central to the healing ministry of Christ. Similar to the African community today, certain rituals, the community, and the centrality of relationships need to be incorporated in the healing processes.

## HEALING AS COMMUNAL AND RELATIONAL EVENT

I agree with the argument put forth by Dube that illnesses such as HIV & AIDS, can be better prevented if approaches to healing them are communally founded. She says:

> Given that HIV & AIDS are symptoms of social ills, it is, therefore, more than an issue of individual morality and health, rather, it is also about morality and health of our cultural, spiritual, economic, and political structures. It is about broken relationships within communities and the world. Given that African Indigenous Religions (AIRs) approach to health and healing is holistic and focuses on the healing of all relationships, it is clear that the African cosmology has a significant contribution to HIV & AIDS prevention. Prevention calls for a community-centered approach in which the whole community works for its own health and the healing of its members.[34]

This is not to say that we ignore all the technological and scientific findings and knowledge available to us; rather, the knowledge has to be contextualized to fit the worldview, values, and systems of those involved. Interventions that ignore the values and norms of those infected and

---

34. Dube, *Adikira*, 145.

affected work for a short while and, thereafter, do not have long lasting effects. In the African context, the way to combat these diseases is to use the everyday lived out cultural worldview–communal. The communities where the intervention has been successful indicate a communal approach to combating the pandemic. Zimbabwe, as an example, having faced economic crisis as other countries globally, is one of those countries that has been able to counter the spread of HIV/AIDS. AVERT (a charity organization in United Kingdom-UK) reports in its research findings that despite Zimbabwe's economic challenges, the rates of new infections have been reduced due to community involvement and education:

> However, regarding HIV and AIDS the country is currently seeing some progress and improvements; Zimbabwe is one of the few countries where incidence has declined by 50 percent between 2001 and 2011. This is partially due to efforts among the population to prevent the spread of HIV, some of which have been remarkable in the context of such immense challenges. Between 2002 and 2006, the population is estimated to have decreased by four million people. The country is now seeing an annual growth rate of 2.2 percent. Average life expectancy is just under 53. By 2011, there were one million children living in Zimbabwe who had been orphaned as a result of parents dying from AIDS. Efforts to prevent the spread of HIV in Zimbabwe have been spearheaded by the NAC (National AIDS Council), non-governmental, religious, and academic organizations. Prevention schemes have been significantly expanded since the turn of the millennium, but remain critically under-funded. Although mortality rates have played a large part in reducing the number of people living with HIV among the population of Zimbabwe, it is believed prevention programmes aimed at behaviour change, and the prevention of mother to child transmission have also been instrumental in bringing about a decline in HIV prevalence.[35]

The findings by AVERT are not isolated to Zimbabwe, but it is now common knowledge that in communally oriented societies, in order to combat a pandemic the best approach is to target changes in communal behaviors and attitudes. It is when most of the community buys into the changes that results and/ or outcomes are noted. In the process of the community working together in the fight against the pandemic, relationships are also formed and strengthened.

35. Avert, *HIV and AIDS in Zimbabwe*, 1.

We find that in the ministry of Christ, healing is holistic (communal, spiritual and psychological) as it is in the African context. Relationships had to be healed and forgiveness had to be pronounced. Graham argues that the modern Western world has compartmentalized the human being. He says:

> This worldview (modern understanding and practice) has been underlying basis for modern medical practice. The body is regarded as a well-ordered machine that functions according to predetermined patterns. Illness is the breakdown of the functioning. Healing consists in establishing the natural functioning or the pro-intervention. These functions can be isolated to the particular parts of the body, with no assumption that there is a connection between all parts, and between the body and its social and physical environment. Neither is it assumed that emotions, mental functions, values, and spiritual capacities play a part in the processes of disease and healing. The person is regarded as an isolated ego inside the body.[36]

In the western worldview, healing seems to occur in a self-contained entity–the individual, whilst in African contexts it involves right relationship with God or other humans, and creation. Any physical and/or sometimes mental illness has some aspects of spiritual ties, so much so that God and/or the spiritual world are involved in the healing processes. Righting of relationships is primary in seeking physical illness. What is believed to make people ill is not limited to one's physical disease, but to how the illness is connected to other aspects of one's well-being, that is, how one lives with others in the community.

It was a shame to the family for an individual to die alone without healthy supportive relationships of one's family and/or at times the whole community. In traditional societies, one never faced illness or death alone. One was born into community, welcomed by the community, and died always surrounded by the community. The saying goes, "even the witch/wizard never dies alone" even one of the most hated members of the community never dies alone. As we look for "best practices" for healing for those infected & affected by HIV/AIDS in sub-Sahara African context, a communal approach to fighting the disease is needed. The policies of confidentiality in Sub-Saharan Africa need to be re-visited and be contextualized to prevent disfranchising individuals, families, and the communities in

---

36. Graham, *Healing,* 499.

trying to prevent the pandemic. The communities that have been found to be successful in fighting against the illness are using communal methods in combating the illness rather than the Western individualistic approaches. Confidentiality tends to be individualistic, and we need an approach that tries to preserve both the individual and community's wellbeing. This type of approach should be easy to adapt since inherently most African contexts are communal by nature. As mentioned earlier, priests or religious leaders of the community need to play a central role in the healing processes.

## RELIGIOUS LEADERS TO TAKE A CENTRAL ROLE, YET REFRAIN FROM ABUSE

HIV/AIDS was one of those diseases that came to the African continent already stigmatized due to its association with sex. The most common way people contract(ed) the disease was through sexual intercourse. This caused many of the church leaders to shun or ridicule anyone who was infected and those affected who were taking care of their beloved. As we have seen in the stories above, Christ's approach to dealing with sin was not "condemnation" but freedom. The theology of care needed is one that draws others to salvation rather than showing them the way to hell. As pastors, we must be bearers of "good news," and showing people the way of salvation. "For the Son of Man (Christ) came to seek and save the ones who are lost" (Luke 19:10). It is well-known and common knowledge that males lead most Christian denominations in sub-Saharan Africa.

It is time for the male pastors to address the subject of HIV/AIDS, and sex (not usually publicly talked about), and let alone from the pulpits. Much is needed from the male pastors in challenging some of the patriarchal attitudes that pose dangerous practices in the face of the pandemic. The days of "boys will be boys" are over; the youth and young men need to be taught African Christian morals and ethics that respect and value life. Given that male pastors are already in the leadership positions, they have much more influence in challenging their male lay counterparts. By willingly spreading the disease, the males are destroying the future of the community.

Lately, the prosperity gospel seems to have taken root in sub-Saharan Africa. Religious leaders (the shepherds) need to be faithful instruments of God, not taking advantage of the their flocks. One of the aspects mentioned earlier is some African people's belief in tangibles such as anointing oil, holy water or small stones, etc., to take home. Some of the church leaders are selling the small rocks, anointing oil and holy water at exorbitant prices to make money instead for the healing rituals. They are taking advantage of the vulnerable and trying to make a profit. Congregants need to be educated that it is not the pastors who does the healing, and neither does the oil, but that it is God who does the healing. God can use the pastors and the material elements in the process as vessel and instruments, but can also do without. The warning in Ezekiel 34 to the priests and shepherds applies to the African context in these days of economic hardships and HIV & AIDS.

> Woe to you shepherds of Israel who only take care of yourselves! Should not shepherds take care of the flock? You eat the curds, clothe yourselves with the wool and slaughter the choice animals, but you do not take care of the flock. You have not strengthened the weak or healed the sick or bound up the injured. You have not brought back the strays or searched for the lost. . . . and because my shepherds did not search for my flock but cared for themselves rather than for my flock, therefore, you shepherds, hear the word of the LORD: . . . I am against the shepherds and will hold them accountable for my flock. I will remove them from tending the flock so that the shepherds can no longer feed themselves. I will rescue my flock from their mouths, and it will no longer be food for them. . . . I myself will tend my sheep and have them lie down, declares the Sovereign LORD. I will search for the lost and bring back the strays. I will bind up the injured and strengthen the weak, but the sleek and the strong I will destroy. I will shepherd the flock with justice.[37]

## HEALING PALAVER RITUALS: INDABAS AND THE TRUTH COMMISSION

Africa, south of the Sahara, has always been known for rituals practices. *Indabas, palavers*[38] *(a formal or informal gathering, open or closed to resolve a crisis)*, similar to "the truth commission," as was done soon after the death of apartheid in South Africa, were modeled after traditional ritual practices. After the horrendous genocides in Rwanda and South Sudan, communities were still able to come together to reconcile and forge a way forward. Wherever life is taken by someone or something, and/or by a disease, this creates

---

37. https://www.biblegateway.com/passage/?search=Ezekiel%2034:1–24
38. Mucherera, *Meet me at the Palaver*, ix.

disharmony in a community. Rituals are needed to bring the environment back into balance and/or cleansing. The rituals performed are not necessarily limited to physical cleansing, but for emotional as well as spiritual cleansing. A dying person (physically) who gets surrounded by relatives where prayer rituals, testimonies, and forgiveness are pronounced dies free emotionally and spiritually. In situations of HIV/AIDS, where a person dying of the illness may be feeling guilty of bringing such an illness into the family, rituals of forgiveness and reconciliation are crucial. It is the work of the pastor and the congregation to necessitate an environment of repentance for the guilty part, and reconciliation leading into ultimate healing for all those involved. A *palaver or indaba* ritual done under the guidance of a caring pastor allows for the facilitation of such healing to occur.

We always have to recognize that beyond the infected, those affected also need a place to openly share their feelings. The open *family or church community palavers* allow for such a safe place and for people to vent their emotions and even anger. What a horrendous or terrible event, for example, for a woman who gets infected unknowingly by a husband, getting shunned by the family or community and being blamed for something that she was not responsible for in the first place.

Those infected or dying of the pandemic still need to be treated as loved children of God, as well as human beings. They are human beings with an infection (as much as they are accountable and still responsible for their choices); it is their humanity (the fact that they are created in the image of God) that counts the most, especially in their last days. Rituals of reconciliation and celebration of their lives are needed so as to set them free as they continue their journey into the world of the living dead. The role of the church is to offer them healing through Christ (spiritual, emotional and social), even though they may not receive the physical cure. It is the "peace that passes all understanding" that church needs to offer them, fully understanding that their physical bodies are returning to dust. The church needs to help offer them freedom through and in Christ, to their souls or spirits, so they can receive their ultimate healing in their final union with the 'cloud of witnesses,' and God.

# Chapter 4

## Conjunction of Gender Violence and HIV/AIDS with Implications for Assessment and Intervention in Pastoral Care

ANNE K. GATOBU, PHD MDIV
ASBURY THEOLOGICAL SEMINARY

HIV/AIDS AND GENDER VIOLENCE? One must wonder what these seemingly two social and moral issues have to do with each other. Given the statistics, the prevalence among certain populations, the social stigma associated with, and the adverse effects onto these populations regarding both HIV/AIDS and Gender Violence, I propose that the incidence of one is reflective of the probability of the other. Indeed, the United Nations has already made this link in their definition of Gender Violence as follows:

> any act of gender-based violence that results in, or is likely to result in, physical, sexual, psychological harm to women, including threats of acts coercion, deprivation of liberty, whether occurring in pubic or private life."[1]

However, their link only alludes to gender violence resulting in the sexual harm of the victim. A more explicit link has been made by the UN's

1. www.who.int/

quest for probabilities for both genders, stating: "Violence against women and girls increase their risk of acquiring HIV."[2]

In this chapter I offer the aspects that explain the conjunction of gender violence with HIV and AIDS. I further dare to propose that the transmission of HIV/AIDS, both in consensual relationships as well as in casual and commercial relationship, should be considered as a form of gender violence with all the aspects of enforceable legal action.

Though many of the examples may be drawn from the African context, it should be noted that the ideologies and concepts discussed herein can be transferable to any context where prevalence of HIV/AIDS is considerable. The choice of the term "Gender Violence" as opposed to "Domestic Violence" is intentional. *Domestic Violence* presumes stable relationships, usually bound by the marriage covenant or other long-term commitment. *Gender Violence*, on the other hand, encompasses both the domestic violence as described above but moves beyond to casual encounters, sexual assault, sex trafficking and any other form of violence vented on another simply by virtue of their gender and vulnerability. The widening of the definitional horizon of gender violence allows the conjunction of HIV/AIDS and gender violence to be explored beyond the confines of long-term relationships. I begin by laying out certain assumptions made from prevalent literature on both HIV/AIDS and Gender Violence, which become the basis for my arguments. I then analyze the statistics, including prevalence with certain populations, and stigma issues to demonstrate that many of the factors that make HIV/AIDS rampant with certain communities and populations in Africa are very similar to factors associated with prevalence of Gender Violence. Indeed, the prevalence of gender violence heightens the probability of HIV/AIDS infection for the female.

In the wake of growing awareness and acceptance by society of homosexual relationships around the world, the term "gender based violence" may begin to lose its meaning and statistical bias. After all, it is reported that lesbian and gay relationships have just as high an incidence of violence as any heterosexual relationship. The considerations of dynamics of violence in the gay and lesbian communities are beyond the considerations of this chapter. Hence, for the sake of the arguments set forth in this chapter, it is critical that gender violence be viewed in the traditional heterosexual relationships because these are where dynamics of violence are documented as basically "power over."

---

2. www.unwomen.org

Whenever gender violence is mentioned, many minds go to such violence being meted by men against women. Reality is that there is gender violence that is meted by women against men. The National Coalition for Domestic Violence (NCADV) reports that 1 out of 5 women are victims of gender violence while 1 out of 7 men are victims of similar abuse.[3] Similar statistics in Africa would significantly multiply the number of women as compared to the number of men who are victims of gender violence. While the difference may be attributed to the cultural demand for men to hide such abuse as it is shameful to them, I believe the statistics would still be very for women in comparison to men. What is more interesting is that very similar lines follow the incidence of HIV/AIDS among women in comparison to men. One wonders if this is a coincidence, or might such statistics be telling us of a strong correlation between Gender Violence and HIV/AIDS? In an interview with Dr. Don Messer, one of the most informed on this issue and an advocate for HIV/AIDs, describes the co-relations in these terms, "Gender violence and HIV/AIDS are two sides of a coin in Africa." I make the argument that these statistics demonstrate patterns that show systemic issues that lead to women being most disadvantaged by both Gender Violence and HIV/AIDS are similar. I also argue that the factors that lead to and sustain both Gender Violence and HIV/AIDS in Africa are not only similar but build on each other.

Of the 25.8 millions of people living with HIV/AIDS in sub Sahara Africa in 2014 (which accounts 70 percent of world HIV/AIDS cases), 56 percent are comprised of new infections amongst women with the proportions being higher for younger women at 66 percent.[4] The same cannot be said of the U.S where, as reported by the Center for Disease Control (CDC), numbers of newly infected women has declined by 40 percent between 2005 and 2014. In reporting the U.S context, the report states that "most new diagnoses in women are attributed to heterosexual sex."[5] This is similar to the African context where most infections are passed through heterosexual sex. Yet, Africa continues to show higher numbers of women infected every year! The fact that the disease has been associated mainly with multiple sexual partners, one must wonder if women in Africa are comparably more promiscuous? The paradoxical reality defies that odd because in many homes, where people have more than one sexual partner

3. www.ncadv.org
4. www.unwomen.org
5. http://www.cdc.gov/hiv/statistics/overview/ataglance.html

or are unfaithful, it is most likely the man and not the woman. Indeed, there is such a strong stigma assigned to a woman who is seen as loose or unfaithful. In traditional Africa, it was not only acceptable but also encouraged for men to have multiple wives. The whole idea of polygamous and concubineship is still a phenomena to be reckoned with in many parts of Africa. The introduction of Christianity had to deal with ingrained mindsets of polygamous Africa. Indeed, one of the biggest challenges that Christianity has had to deal with as converts flock into churches is what to do with families where men have more than one wife.[6] Arguing that the church has to find ways to embrace the people that have accepted Christ after many years of being in polygamous marriages, Majembe states that churches cannot just reject such people or ask them to divorce their wives.[7] In this same African context, the unfaithfulness of a wife to a husband by even showing interest in another other was enough to call for divorce. Women were, and continue to be, held at a higher standard of faithfulness than men–so much so that even in Christian circles there is greater toleration for a man to be promiscuous than a woman. The stigma that is attached to promiscuity for a woman, especially a married woman, is so adverse that it is enough to curtail such aspirations. Furthermore, women socialized to be family nurturers have much more to loose than their counterpart men when it comes to promiscuity. They stand to loose face in the society, identity as a wife, social standing as a woman of worth, their children, and even their property, which is usually vicariously owned through their husbands. It is true that the society has considerably changed and we are no longer living in traditional Africa in the more industrialized and westernized regions of Africa. Yet, the idea of sanctity and purity being a prize for female identity continues to run strong, such that a considerable number of women will be extremely mindful of multiple sexual partners. All this to say, the statistics of women being the most infected by HIV/AIDS just does not add up. Would it then be accurate to say that most women who contract HIV/AIDS from their sexual partners, whether married or single are victims of sexual demands that if they had the power to say 'NO,' they could? Making the statement, Dr. Messer states:

> Women lack self-autonomy over their own bodies. They often are not free to resist sexual overtures because of the threat or actuality of violence. Poverty further complicates this situation since older

6. Mucherera, *Pastoral Care*.
7. Majembe, *A Study to Identify*.

men take advantage of younger women, becoming "sugar daddies" that offer young women money for food or clothing or tuition. Statistics demonstrate that younger women tend to get HIV from older men. The women likewise are unable to protect themselves sexually, since men are famous for resisting the use of condoms because they insist it reduces their "pleasure."[8]

Women in many parts of the continent do not have equal rights in the society and are often treated as second-class citizens. They are, thus, generally susceptible to subjugation, suppressions, and acts of violence. In many African countries, women do not inherit any landed property and in some cases cannot even own property except jointly with their husbands or brother. This leaves them in helpless situations that demand subservience even in the most unconstitutional situations. Messer points to the salient status of women in Africa and many other non-western cultures saying,

> The secondary and stigmatized status of women is often internalized so that women come to believe that it is OK for husbands to beat their wives, if the wives resist sexual advances or even cook a less than perfect meal. Maria Cimperman (a Roman Catholic nun and academic ethicist) writes in "When God's People Have HIV and AIDS" writes extensively about gender violence in Africa. Her studies in Zambia were astounding and sad. Eighty percent of the women found it acceptable to be beaten by husbands "as a form of chastisement."[9]

In some subcultures, widows are inherited by the brother of their deceased husband in the name of offering her protection since she cannot own property on her own and only belonged to the family home through her now deceased husband. She is expected to have sex with the husband's older brothers since he now has inherited her. Besides the indignity associated with such inheritance, the chances of HIV infection multiplies due to the multiple sexual relationship partnership that the death of her husband has resulted in. Discussing this phenomenon, Naitore Nthurima, a graduate of Marriage & Family Counseling Program from Asbury Theological Seminary and native of Kenya, states,

> Certain cultural traditions continue to increase the number of those who get infected with HIV/AIDS. Wife inheritance occurs when the husband of a woman dies and the woman gets passed

8. Messer Interview, 8–31-16.
9. Messer interview 8–31-16.

on to her late husband's brother who will marry her as his second/third wife and is responsible to carry on the name of his late brother and will bring up any children in his brother's name. This tradition tends so encourage the increase of HIV/AIDS in cases where the late brother died of HIV/AIDS complications and having infected his wife, her new husband ends up getting infected and eventually his first wife too. Tradition trumps everything including sickness. In this case, both woman and man are at risk of getting infected. Gender violence comes in when the woman is unwilling to get passed on to her brother-in-law as well as when the first wife does not have a say in what her husband does. Both women are expected to fulfill their conjugal responsibilities to the man.[10]

Naitore's statement is on target with regard to the incidence of women subjugation being directly related to HIV/AIDS contraction. Viewed from this argument, it is clear that the spread of HIV/AIDS among women in Africa is really heightened by gender and sexual violence, vulnerability, and lack of rights.

More profound is the prevalence and rampancy of HIV/AIDS among girls between age 15 and 24 years, meaning mainly unmarried women. It is estimated that in 2013 alone, there were 380,000 new infections in this age group.[11] In 2015 there was an estimated 2.3 million adolescent girls and young women living with HIV/AIDS, constituting 60 percent of all people living with HIV/AIDS. The figures for new infections in 2015 are even higher for this age group of females at 66 percent.[12] So how do these girls get infected by HIV/AIDS if not through rape and sexual trafficking? In the Industrialized regions, one will argue that girls have lost their moral virtues associated with sexuality. Yet, that is only a small percentage of the girl population because the greater percentage knows that their security for marriage and lifelong partnerships depends on their virginity and moral uprightness! That is the reality of the life of girls in Africa. Yet, they are high in numbers of those living with HIV/AIDS. So then how does one explain the anomaly? Rape is the number one explanation. Most girls, because of the dynamics of households and vulnerability, are raped between the ages of 5 and 18. Such rapes are not only committed by their age mates (in the case of teenager) but also by older men, which is generally accepted in the

10. Naitore Interview 8–29-16.
11. www.avert.org
12. www.unwomen.org

household in the name of extended families. Many girls fall prey to uncles and so-called cousins, who half the time are not even blood relatives but persons incorporated into the family by association or proximity. Young girls become easy prey because they learn to trust these uncles and cousins. With the breakdown of familial education about sex and adulthood, most of the girls are not even aware that they have been violated till they grow older. Where they know that they have been violated, many do not feel they have the avenue to report such violation because the society's stances to keep secrets of such happening due to its repercussions to the rest of the family. It is not until they are of age and test for HIV/AIDs that many of them realize that their violations also came with a death sentence! Who would argue against perceiving this as gender violence?

Rape is also rampant in the war torn zones of Africa like Somalia, Northern Kenya, the DRC, and parts of West Africa. Soldiers and rebels alike have been known to burst into villages, usually populated by women and children since the men are out in the wars. They take young women to serve them physically and sexually in their hiding. Indeed, rape is intentionally used as a *"weapon of war"* in these war torn regions. Traditionally, when tribes went to war with one another, part of their main "spoil" that they carried back home as trophies was the young women who then served as wives and farmhands in their homes. Indeed, when many of us trace our ancestral lines we find evidence of this traditional practice by inter-marriages of women who cannot identify their real areas of immigrations as they were brought to the community at very young ages. It is unfortunate that none of these have been documented and the only evidence is the features, names, frames, and oral stories of families who clearly had grandparents that were inter marriage in far off tribes. Today the tides have changed. The scene is more violent because in the traditional society even though women were carried of as part of the propertied spoil, they were not harmed and would usually be married off in their new communities. Today's scene is pure war rape just for pleasure and release. Hence, there is no investment in the life of the women who is being used as a sex object, no relationship, and no accountability. Reports of multiple soldiers raping one or two women in mass rapes are not new. What I describe here is an uncensored context where infection of HIV/AIDS would thrive and spread like fire. And then we wonder if all these women contracting HIV/AIDS are that promiscuous!

War-torn regions are also characterized by refugee camps. When populations of people are removed from their homes due to civil wars in the regions, many are resettled in refugee camps, which have little in form of recourse and laws. Young girls become prey of both the men in the refugee camps as well as the soldiers and guerillas who have no other long-term commitments. Even as I describe this scene, it occurs to me that I am painting a very glum picture of immorality and almost beastlike behavior. Yet, the truth is that these are the ravages of wars. Wars and civil wars have a way of transforming well abiding and even God-fearing citizens into animals where people disconnect with their human instincts and embrace animal instincts. Once again, how can society not see the manifestation of HIV/AIDs contraction from war torn areas as anything other than repercussions of gender based violence? While boys are also caught in similar war mayhem, they are less vulnerable than their counterpart girls. So even if violence is meted to all, gender selective violence does result in sexual molestation and incidence of HIV/AIDS among women than men.

The issue of Female Genital Mutilation [FGM] is not new in many parts of Africa. According to a UN statistic, at least 200 million women living today have undergone FGM in 30 countries, and it may be assumed that most of these are in Africa.[13] Though many non-profits and religious organizations have worked hard to try and eradicate this archaic tradition that endangers the health of girls around Africa, its prevalence is still astronomical. The numbers that seem to lessen are mainly indicative of a tradition gone underground to escape the scrutiny of government and other legal entities. The practice is very much alive, especially in sections of the continent, which are less exposed to westernization. Its prevalence ranges from about 5 percent to 90 percent! Such variation reflects regions that have embraced westernization (especially formal education) and industrialization. Regions that still hold dear to traditional gendered values, and regions that are war torn see the very high percentages of the prevalence of this practice. It is proven that FGM has no beneficial value to the girls. Its only value is to sexually benefit the male partners while curtailing sexual enjoyment of the female. As Messer states in an interview, "women everywhere are more susceptible biologically to getting infected. When violence is involved, vaginal or anal tearing can easily occur making the probability of infection even greater." Messer is right in pointing to the vulnerability of

---

13. www.unwomen.org

women in general to HIV/AIDS infection. The incidence of FGM heightens that vulnerability both biologically and socially.

FGM also signals to the society in many parts of Africa, that now the girl is ready for marriage. The very intention and impact of FGM on girls is an act of violence. That coupled with the signal for readiness of sexual relationship, even though the girl may not be psychologically or socially ready, is in itself a violation of human rights and an exposure to vulnerability of preying men. There is also no telling how many girls who undergo FGM in non-sanitary contexts contract HIV/AIDS because of the uncensored contact of blood. All these are factors that magnify the chances of such young girls contracting HIV/AIDS at a very early age and under no informed consent of their own. How else can one view such acts of physical, psychological, and emotional mutilations of girls except as gender violence!

Economic disadvantage and, therefore, poverty levels of many women in Africa is yet another factor that contributes to the two-sided coin of Gender Violence and HIV/AIDS. As Messer states,

> Around the world I have met with sex workers, who almost always are uneducated women with children, with no other way to earn income. They are in my eyes engaged in survival sex, far more sinned against than sinners.[14]

The best example of such a disadvantaged economic status is the well known yet least documented phenomenon in Africa–house-girls, generally known as "maids" in most African homes. The status of house-girls in the society generally heightens their vulnerability to violence. Abuse of power over house-girls is very real and detrimentally harmful. I am intentionally talking of *house girls* as opposed to *houseboys* whom I briefly discuss in the next paragraph, as the latter pose a different challenge. House girls are among the lowest in social status simply because they are less educated, have less skilled resources than the average citizen, and are usually from very economically low homes. I know anyone reading this may think that is such a condescending attitude towards house-girls, and yet, it is a reality that helps make my point about their vulnerability. Were it not so, there would be many women aspiring for a career to be a house girl. Many of these young girls who get into this "profession" do so because of need, either they have a child or two at home to support, or aging parents or other family members who rely on them, or because they have come to an end of

---

14. Messer Interview 8-31-16.

their formal education usually because of lack of fees, or because they did not do well in school and had to drop out. A considerable percentage of these young girls did not go to any higher levels of school beyond elementary due to lack of access to education. For many of them their parents have to make "tough" choices about which child to send to school and which child will have to remain home because of economic hardships. Without fail, when such a decision has to be made, girls are disadvantaged because of patriarchal values and the belief that she will be taken care of through marriage. Hence, the young girls find themselves in the big cities many times coming directly from the village, living in a strange home where they literally run the homes under undesirable conditions. They have no power and no voice, since they do not necessarily belong in these homes. In these same homes are many men who, as already described, view the female as a sexual object simply because of their gender. Many times, because of and at times even despite the good relationship between man and his wife, the house girls end up giving not only household chore services but also sexual services to the men in the home. And they have to keep it secret because, should the lady of the house find out of the extra-service, they become a double victim by losing their job and security in the home. Such sexual abuse may, therefore, go unknown for years. Well, any man who would go so low as to have sexual relationship with his house girl behind the back of the wife would be expected to have other relationships outside of the marriage covenant. Similarly, many of the sexually abused house-girls may try to drown their pain of abuse they cannot talk about by finding other relationships outside the home, in the community. As sexual molestation literature tells us, disregard for self due to pain and abuse can lead to self hate and devaluation so much so that they do not really have any qualms about offering their bodies to anyone who would affirm them. What I describe is a vicious cycle that now stands the likelihood of spreading HIV/AIDS to a whole host of people involved. I wonder if the context described above would not fit the bill of gender violence and also a ripe context for HIV/AIDS!

If the stones were turned and the house-help is a man, normally referred to as houseboy, the vulnerability significantly changes. Indeed, I am yet to meet one houseboy who, even though living under similar conditions of poor pay, less respect, and low economic and educational backgrounds, has been vulnerable to sexual abuse. Indeed, the stones turn so dramatically that if there are any young girls in the house, there is every possibility that these young girls could be in danger of being raped by the houseboys. In fact, reports of houseboys who have violated young girls as young as five years old are rampant. After all, children are left in the care of house-helps, whether men or women, for long hours while the two parents work outside of home.

The grim picture painted of house-help both as victims of sexual abuse (in the case of girls) and perpetrators of abuse (generally as men), has made many parents take a proactive stance of extreme vetting of their house-help and treating them with mistrust. Many households now prefer to have someone only come to clean the house, wash clothes, or cook and then leave. Yet, it does not fully eliminate the fact that they have full access to the home in the absence of parents and children can still be vulnerable to preying men who can come and go any time of the day since it is also their home. It must be noted that just as much as the house-helps need these jobs to provide for themselves in economies where jobs are scarce and unemployment is high, the households heavily rely on this help. Even if one can have all the chores taken care of by a day-worker who does not live in the home, they need someone to be in the house while they are away due to insecurity and the high probability of homes being broken into while people are at work. Hence, each party somehow needs the other. Indeed, for Africans living in diaspora in the Western countries, the luxury of affordable house-help is one that almost everyone cites they miss about being back in Africa. Only recently in Kenya laws were passed to protect house-helps from abuse of low pay by instituting a minimum wage for them. Hopefully this will redeem the profession and give confidence, hope, and a voice to those living in dire abusive conditions. To give credit, many well wishing house-help employers have every intention to "assist" their house-help to move beyond the vicious non-opportunity employment as a house-help by offering them strategies and means to get some education or skill training that would enable them to establish themselves in other trades other than house-help. Maybe these few well-intentioned employers and the institution of broader protective laws for house-help are what might truly give voice to those caught in the chains of abuse.

Lack of access to educational insight and actual preventive resources for sexual intercourse, like condoms, are a huge contributor to HIV/AIDS contraction. In many African societies, the resistance to the use of condoms is both theological and also politically based gender oppression. As Messer rightly states,

> In my travels I have often been in church conferences where male pastors and theologians denounce the use of condoms, but it is rare indeed when a woman speaks negatively about condoms. Women have so few means of protection that they understand their value and importance, not just in terms of pregnancy but in terms of protection from various diseases, especially HIV and other sexually transmitted illnesses.[15]

Expressing similar sentiments, Naitore asks a provocative question, Could gender violence be psychological? A woman has no say as to whether she or her husband uses protection during sexual intercourse. There is an underlying belief that sex is purely for the man. The woman is not an equal partner and so she is left at the mercy of the man, be it her husband or any man who yields power over her.[16]

Naitore's statement demonstrates that gender violence does not have to be physical to be linked to HIV/AIDS. The psychological suppression that demeans the woman to the point of believing and, thereby, responding to inhuman demands on her, are indicative of the reality of conjunction between gender based violence and HIV/AIDS.

## IMPLICATIONS FOR ASSESSMENT AND INTERVENTION

In the foregoing section I have argued for the consideration of HIV/AIDS as a form of gender violence at least in its spread and contraction by women–both elderly and young. If persuaded so, one must complete the loop by asking what then are the implication of this in assessment and intervention? Below I offer a number of observations for both assessment and intervention to break the cycle.

If indeed contraction of HIV/AIDS by women is enhanced by the general vulnerability of women, empowerment of women in all sectors of the continent is one of the most effective solutions. Women must be empowered to perceive themselves as good, contributing, and outstanding citizens. They must understand and perceive themselves not as second-class citizens but as children of God with full rights of every human being. Such confidence may come about through the mirroring of oneself to God. The transformation that happens in such mirroring is internal and wells-up

15. Messer Interview, 8-31-16.
16. Naitore Interview 8-29-16.

from the inside to produce a self-differentiated individual that can call to accountability and challenge systems that maintain the status quo. Such a self can defy the secretive nature of abusive relationships or redefine her role in maintaining the abuse. This work would be best done through individual counseling and community empowerment initiatives.

One of the most powerful approaches to women empowerment, either in pastoral counseling or group encounters, is the narrative approach proposed by Michael White.[17] This approach works very well in multicultural contexts and especially oral cultures like Africa where the stories, saying, proverbs, and folklores are powerful tools for lessons and empowerment. In this approach, women are able to tell their stories in their own language, pace, and vocabulary, thus revealing negative strongholds that have dominated a metanarrative of defeat and victimization. The facilitators (hosts) of such would then invite open questions and use pointers that work to deconstruct the false bedrocks of their stories. For instance, many women believe that they do not have economic power in their own homes and perceive the male partners as the sole providers, so much so that they believe the family cannot survive without male provision. Reality, based on research conducted with women living in gender violence relationships in Kenya, reveals that most of these gender violence violated homes are actually run and provided for by the meager earnings of the woman who is the main hustler in the home. Most of the men in such violent prone relationships, who might actually earn big money and thus be perceived as the breadwinner for the family, may as a matter of fact contribute little or nothing to the financial well being of the family.[18] Open questions that help the women process who really is providing for the family may be what are needed to completely deconstruct her narrative and the man's role towards welfare of the family. Once a pointed and cognitive shift is made, the host can then facilitate the reconstruction of narratives that hold the proactive and creative things that the women engage in for the survival of their family. These become the new empowering and hopeful scaffolds that hold their new metanarrative.

A second, and closely related intervention for HIV/AIDS, is the need to dismantle patriarchal systems that continue to fuel and maintain the gender violence and breed the perfect contexts for HIV/AIDS to thrive. This initiative requires a much larger intervention strategy as it demands a

17. Nichols, *Family Therapy*.
18. Gatobu, *Female Identity Formation*.

systemic approach. The maintenance of sociopolitical and cultural systems that continue to oppress citizens simply by their gender is not only archaic but the cancer that will continue to eat into the woman's health psychologically, physically, and mentally. In a different work I have argued that the major reason why gender based violence continues to plague and be sustained in Africa is patriarchal systems that demand women to form female identities that be-little them and make them perceive themselves as second place citizens. Hence, when they experience gender violence, they accept it as fate, or as normative for what it means to be a female in that society.[19] It is a very close concept to what Cross as well as Morten and Atkinson propose in the minority cultural development in the U.S where many minorities are stuck in a self hate stage because of systems in place that demand they perceive their culture and race as less than by holding the Caucasian race as the yardstick for what is normative.[20]

Last, and maybe most important, is that assessments for HIV/AIDS should not be done on the superficial level of testing only. It should be supplemented by assessment for gender-based violence so as to move the solutions to a more systemic outlook of the epidemic. This would not only lead to more effective intervention strategies but also begin to address issues of stigma by affecting communities of survivors. The current model of intervention for HIV/AIDS is to distribute antiretroviral medication to sustain the infected and to counsel them when they face stigma. While these are very necessary interventional approaches, they leave the survivor vulnerable to an even greater risk of psychological suffering. She has to somehow live in a community that stigmatizes her and shuns her as a member of the community. For many infected persons in Africa, this indeed is the hardest phase of dealing with their disease. How empowering, healing, and therapeutic could it be if the holding environment of the survivor were positively affected to embrace her and help her rehabilitate into the community. This is not a new measure by any means. Systems theory came to be because of the practitioner's realization that patients who had been hospitalized for illnesses like Schizophrenia thrived in the hospital environment because of the hospital family that provided an embracing, accepting, and therapeutic community. As soon as they went back to their original systems, homeostatic forces kicked in to re-mold a perfectly well

---

19. Gatobu, *Female Identity Formation*.
20. Morten and Atkinson, *Minority Identity Development*, 156–161.

individual into a schizophrenic patient all over again.[21] The same applies to survivors of HIV/AIDS. If not removed from the violent prone environments and the negative stigma-laden communities, they are bound to let go of their newly empowered narratives and revert back to their victimized role. Hence, the importance of transforming patriarchal systems to systems that are committed to gender mutuality cannot be understated.

---

21. Nichols, *Family Therapy*, 12.

# Chapter 5

## Healing Postcolonial Trauma in the African Experience
*The Case of D.R. Congo*

### M. FULGENCE NYENGELE, PHD
METHODIST THEOLOGICAL SCHOOL IN OHIO

COLONIALISM IS A PRACTICE of domination, which involves the use of force to subjugate one group of people to another.[1] It is inherently violent because the very process of conquest, control, and the practice of political and economic domination that characterize colonialism are all acts of violence. Colonialism establishes a relationship of control and influence, which is socially manifested by the formation of a hierarchical system with a settler class at the top followed by a local elite class, and a lower class constituted by the masses or various indigenous peoples who are controlled by the settler class with the assistance of the local elite class. Inherent in such a system are notions of racial superiority and inferiority, as well as exotic otherness that are used to justify the subjugation.[2] The essence of colonialism then is the direct and overall control and subordination of one group or nation to another not only on the basis of state power being in the hands of a dominating alien power, but also in the use of violence to conquer,

---

1. See "Colonialism," *Stanford Encyclopedia of Philosophy*.
2. Dirlik, *Rethinking Colonialism*, 428–448.

control, and subdue.³ As Juan Rapadas suggests, "the act of taking over and conquering a land and its people is never a peaceful endeavor and is almost always accompanied by violence, subjugation, and dehumanization."⁴ Political domination is secured by force and consequently inflicts trauma in the process.

Historians of colonialism in Africa have suggested that, while European colonization was a brutal enterprise characterized by vicious and cruel treatment of Africans, the Democratic Republic of Congo "has had one of the most violent and unhappy colonial histories of any [country] on the African continent."⁵ Arguing that it would not be difficult to view the history of colonialism in Africa as nothing but a catalogue of cruelty, exploitation and depredation, Anthony Daniels observes that the worst example was probably King Leopold's Congo.⁶ Yet, parts of that history have become better known only in recent years.⁷ We are learning that the Congolese people were not only conquered, dominated, and colonized by the Belgians—they were not only wounded and devastated by the colonial violence they experienced—but that they were also deeply demoralized, abused, and dehumanized. In fact, King Leopold of Belgium, who owned and ruled the Congo as his personal property from the 1870s to 1908, literally converted the country into a giant forced labor camp, where his army and colonial administration forced the Congolese to extract ivory, hardwoods, and wild rubber in enormous amounts and for commercial purposes, with terrible consequences to the health and well-being of Congolese women, men, children, and their communities.⁸

Many people were beaten to death for failing to meet strict quotas of rubber, ivory, or any other commodity they were required to supply, and millions of people died from physical exhaustion and famine. Mass killings, executions, torture, kidnappings, severed hands, taking hostages, in addition to forced labor as noted above, were the order of the day.⁹ These practices led to the decimation of entire villages and communities. Congolese

---

3. Adapted from Rapadas, *Transmission of Violence*, 33–40; Dirlik, "Rethinking Colonialism," 430.
4. Rapadas, *Transmission of Violence*, 33–40.
5. Hochschild, "Introduction," in Marchal, *Lord Leverhulme's Ghosts*, vii.
6. Daniels, *Western Perceptions*, 166.
7. Hochschild, *King Leopold's Ghost*, 164.
8. Ibid., 164.
9. Ibid., 160–165, 254–280.

historian Osumaka Likaka, for example, writes about extremely degrading and inhuman ways in which rubber companies exported tons of rubber, ivory, palm oil products, and hides "while leaving behind emptied villages, particularly in the inner Congo Basin where heavy population losses occurred that disrupted and sometimes destroyed the village communities."[10] Embarrassed by international revelations of atrocities committed by King Leopold's rule in the Congo, the Belgian parliament voted to take the Congo as a Belgian colony in 1908. But similar humiliating practices and maltreatment of the Congolese continued, although to some extent less severe than the harsh practices of King Leopold. But the punishment suffered by the Congolese for not producing expected amounts of needed commodities like cotton, or not working the number of hours required when building roads or working in construction jobs or mining, was still extreme and inhuman; people received hundred or more lashes on their bare buttocks and in the presence of their families and friends, as punishment for not working hard enough or not producing the requisite amount of a needed commodity. Colonial physical punishment was still a public event for all to see. These practices, albeit in some modified forms, were replicated during the thirty-two years of Mobutu Sese Seko's dictatorship that followed the acquisition of independence from Belgium in 1960. Indeed, Mobutu severely punished his political opponents and, in the early years of his reign, hanged his enemies publically for all to see. Ashis Nandy, in his book on the loss and recovery of self under colonialism, is correct when he suggests that "what others can do to you, you also can do to your own kind."[11] Asserting that in postcolonial settings the colonial mantle is now worn by native regimes, he suggests that these postcolonial elites are "willing to do what the colonial powers did," as they repress and mistreat their own people. And this is clearly evidence that colonization has significant deleterious effects on the psyche of the colonized. The colonized can internalize a distorted view of the world and of themselves and, as a consequence, begin to reenact historical injustices that inflict wounds on themselves and on their own people. Rather than being an external reality, political control and subjugation becomes internal to the psyche of the colonized; it becomes internalized colonization—a result of colonial violence. This phenomenon, as a manifestation of postcolonial trauma, can be transmitted from generation to generation, if it is not acknowledged and interrupted.

10. Likaka, *Naming Colonialism*, 32.
11. Nandy, *The Intimate Enemy*, 11–16.

Postcolonial trauma is a pervasive reality in countries that were formerly colonized and groups that were conquered, subjugated, and dominated.[12] While some countries affected by colonization have identified and processed the collective losses incurred under colonial conquest and rule and, therefore, have been able to mourn these losses and begin to chart a healthier course for their people, the Democratic Republic of Congo (D.R.C.) has been peculiarly silent about its brutal history and, thus, has not yet collectively sought to understand the recurring political violence, social instability, and armed conflicts as reenactments of its grossly brutal colonial past.

This chapter will explore aspects of colonial violence in Congolese history in order to gain understanding of the relationship between colonial violence and the suffering caused by recurring patterns of social instability and political violence. The focus will be on identifying aspects of colonial trauma and to explore ways that these are transmitted from generation to generation, as they are reenacted and replicated in contemporary Congolese life. Postcolonial trauma will be described as a form of internalized colonization that continues to oppress and brutalize Congolese life. This effort is, among other things, an attempt not only to memorialize these painful and traumatic collective experiences, but also begin to explore and identify resources and practices for the transformation of Congolese collective consciousness and, therefore, contribute to the renewal and empowerment of Congolese collective imagination toward healing and the facilitation of human flourishing. There is a profound need to create a new Congolese society that does not replicate the horrendous historical injustices suffered under colonial rule and the ensuing dictatorship years, or reenact leadership styles and societal patterns and behaviors that continue to carry or transmit postcolonial trauma. A breach with a brutal colonial past and the consequent healing of postcolonial trauma is possible.

---

12. While this phenomenon can also be applied to countries that colonized other countries, as these countries can suffer from the aftermath or effects of no longer functioning as colonizing forces, some postcolonial theorists have coined the term "postcolonial melancholia" as a more appropriate term to describe the loss of empire, imperial power, dominance, and pre-eminence. Howe, *Internal Decolonization?* 286–304.

## WHAT IS POSTCOLONIAL TRAUMA?

Before describing what postcolonial trauma is, it is important to define the term *trauma*. Judith Herman has characterized the core experience of trauma as terror and disconnection. She describes psychological traumas as "an affliction of the powerless. . . . [in which] the victim is rendered helpless by overwhelming force."[13] Herman conceptualizes the experience of terror as involving disempowerment, helplessness, and abandonment, and she sees in disconnection a sense of shattered trust, as one has experienced a traumatic event. A traumatic situation is an intense experience that involves life threatening aspects, an overwhelming sense of powerlessness, and a change in worldview.[14] There can also be a loss of the assumptive world as the assumptions one had about the world, safety, or people are challenged and undermined by the event. However, it should be noted that, while some definitions of trauma describe traumatic events as outside the range of regular human experience, Herman argues that traumatic events are a common part of human experience, including war, sexual and domestic violence, and child abuse.[15] The following pages will show that Belgian colonization involved terror and significant life threatening aspects, provoking an overwhelming sense of powerlessness on the part of the Congolese people, and a change in worldview in several instances. For example, because of the harsh treatment they were receiving under the colonial rule of King Leopold II, many Congolese women started to refuse to have children. They did not want to bring children in such a hostile environment and inhospitable world. Clearly, there was a shattering of assumptions and belief system about the world that led to the decision to not have children during early colonial times in the Congo. Their sense of trust shattered. On the basis of this discussion, postcolonial trauma can simply be defined as trauma stemming from colonialism, with its inherent violence and trauma causing colonial practices.

David Becker also provides descriptions of trauma that are helpful for our purposes. He suggests that trauma "implies a notion of tearing, of rupture, [disruption], of structural breakdown."[16] He goes on to say that, "trauma can only be defined and understood with reference to a specific

---

13. Herman, *Trauma and Recovery*, 33.
14. Ibid., 1–2.
15. Ibid., 88.
16. Becker, *Dealing with the Consequences*, 33.

context, which should be described in detail."[17] Becker also adds that trauma is a process that develops sequentially and contains both an individual intrapsychic dimension and a collective, macro-social dimension that are interwoven.[18] Following Becker's suggestion, I will try to provide a detailed description of the Congolese colonial context and experience of colonial trauma, and I will focus more on the collective and macro-dimension of the Congolese colonial experience. I focus on the collective and macro-dimension of colonial trauma because colonial trauma is collective trauma in that it reflects, [19] in the case of the Congo, an ongoing chronic condition of recurring violence and political instability—in the form of recurring wars and armed conflicts since independence in 1960. Sociologist Kai Erickson defines collective trauma as a "blow to the basic issues of social life that damages the bonds attaching people together and impairs the prevailing sense of community."[20] The transmission of colonial trauma from generation to generation continues to reenact the ruptures in social life suffered during colonial times and to replicate the dynamics of social unrest wrought by colonialism. The historical injustices and wounds suffered in colonial times are being replicated in contemporary Congolese life. This collective trauma has become part of the Congolese culture and collective psyche, and thus has turned into what Jeffrey C. Alexander and Neil J. Smelser have identified as "cultural trauma.[21] And one might say that there is an ongoing culture of social pain that is being transmitted from generation to generation. Erickson, commenting on the nature and dynamics of collective trauma, goes on to suggest that "the experience of trauma, at its worst, can mean not only a loss of confidence in the self but also in the scaffolding of family and community, in the structures of human government, in the larger logics by which humankind lives, and in the ways of nature itself."[22] Clearly, the words tearing, rupture, disruption, and structural breakdown noted by Becker, and the blow to social life and impairing the sense of community noted by Erickson, describe the colonial experience of Congolese people, who did not only see the tearing down and disruption of family

17. Ibid., 2.
18. Ibid., 33.
19. Alexander, "Toward a Theory of Cultural Trauma," 1–30.
20. Erickson, *A New Species of Trouble*, 233.
21. When trauma becomes an integral part of the culture, it becomes cultural trauma. Smelser, *"Psychological Trauma,"* 31–111.
22. Erickson, *A New Species of Trouble*, 242.; Leveton, *Healing Collective Trauma*.

and community life and the breakdown of their social and political institutions, but also literally experienced the devastation and destruction of their bodies through harsh physical punishments strategically administered and reinforced in order to break any resistance to colonial power and to force people into compliance with colonial rule.

Again, following this discussion, postcolonial trauma can be described as a collective condition of traumatization suffered by a group of people as a result of colonization. As an injury and tear in the social and psychic fabric, the experience of postcolonial trauma occurs within a social, historical, and political context where past experiences of colonial oppression are internalized and continue to be reenacted and replicated in the behaviors of individuals, institutions, and nations. It is a condition where recent or past histories of people are replete with some or all of the following: violence, death, rape, torture, dehumanization, loss of land, culture, and spirit.[23] Throughout its recent and past histories, the DRC has known a lot of violence, death, rape, torture, dehumanization, is still suffering from the effects of armed conflicts fueled by armed groups engaged in illicit trade in natural resources.[24]

Acknowledging this reality and beginning to identify links between contemporary manifestations of colonial trauma and events in the colonial past would be an important step in the search for strategies to interrupt the transmission of this trauma to future generations.

---

23. Rapadas, 34. I think it is appropriate here to say that the DSM definition of trauma as PTSD, as helpful as it is in working with individuals and families who are traumatized, it was not meant to describe whole communities, cultures, or national experiences of colonial violence and trauma. The PTSD diagnosis cannot fully capture and help conceptualize the collective suffering of the victims of colonial violence. So, there are those who have suggested that there is a need to develop a diagnosis label or nomenclature that describes a condition where recent and past histories of people are replete with violence, death, rape, torture,, dehumanization, loss of land, culture, language, and spirit—which is a condition that seems to describe all the experiences of indigenous, colonized peoples. And so some people suggest labels such as "rippled PTSD" to describe the effects of a stone dropped into a pool; "postcolonial stress disorder" (PCSD), "post-trauma transmission disorder" (PTTD), or "postcolonial traumatic syndrome." But there is no consensus that I am aware of at this point, and there is still more work to be done to come up with an adequate description of the effects of colonial violence on individuals, communities, and nations. PTSD is just too inadequate to capture that reality.

24. Mukwege, *Tracing the Source*.

## D.R. CONGO'S VIOLENT COLONIAL PAST

American historian Adam Hochschild suggests that much of the history of central Africa, and the Congo in particular, is "a story of atrocities hidden from view, of white men in Africa portraying themselves to the world as philanthropists, of human suffering that lay behind [products that] millions of Europeans and Americans [use] daily, and, above all, a story of forced labor."[25] Indeed, the colonization of the Congo was a notorious slave labor system run by King Leopold II of Belgium and his successors, and by private companies whose primary interest was the extraction of the Congolese resources for their own benefit, without ever investing in the country itself.[26] Colonialism inflicted massive human suffering in the Congo. In fact, to say that Congo is a country deeply marked by colonial violence and trauma is perhaps a serious understatement. A brief historical account would be helpful for our discussion.

The first contact between Europeans and Congolese people started in 1482, when the Portuguese sailor Diego Cao "discovered" the mouth of the Congo River.[27] Soon after that, missionaries, soldiers, traders, and explorers followed; and by several decades later thousands of Africans were being shipped every year as slaves from this area to the New World. In 1506, the then King of the Kongo Kingdom by the name of Nzinga Mbemba converted to Christianity and took on the Christian name of Affonso. But during nearly 40 years of his rule, he saw his kingdom decimated by the slave trade. There are very good records of the letters that Affonso wrote to the successive kings of Portugal, pleading for putting an end to the slave trade and other atrocities that were being committed by Europeans.

In one of his letters in 1526, Affonso wrote in desperation the following words to King Joao III of Portugal: "each day, the traders are kidnapping our people—children of this country, sons of our nobles and vassals, even people of our own family . . . Our land is entirely depopulated."[28] But there

---

25. Hochschild, *"Introduction,"* vii.

26. Ibid., viii.

27. I am indebted to the following sources on this section: Hochschild, *King Leopold's Ghost*; Lieve Spaas, *How Belgium Colonized the Mind of the Congo* (Edwin Mellen Press, 2007); Ndaywell, *Histoire Generale du Congo*; and Jules Marchal, *L'Histoire du Congo 1910–1945*. Tome 1 (Borgloon: Editions Paula Bellings, 1999).

28. Hochschild, *"Introduction,"* p.viii. Hochschild suggests that Affonso's letters in Portuguese are considered to be the first known documents written by a black African in a European language.

was no response to Affonso's pleas. For several centuries the Atlantic slave trade continued to victimize both the people of his kingdom and Africans living hundreds of miles into the interior. "Several million Africans were taken from this region around the Congo river's mouth mainly to work on the plantations of Brazil [and other parts of South America and in Central America]."[29] In this sense, the first commodity to be extracted from the Congo were human beings. Europeans happily justified the slave trade by saying that they were introducing Africans to civilization, the dignity of labor, and Christianity. In fact, before the captured slaves were taken to the New World, they were often baptized and given Christian names.

With the end of the Atlantic slave trade in the middle of the 19th century, "the major part of Europe's conquest and colonization of Africa began." Historians have characterized this conquest, often called the "scramble for Africa," as "one of the greatest land grabs in history—and one of the swiftest." Again, there is a growing consensus among many historians of European colonization in Africa that "the bloodiest single phase of Africa's colonization was centered on the territory [now known] as [the Democratic Republic of Congo]."[30] Congolese historian Ndaywell even argues that the rubber boom of the 1890s was "the saddest page in the history of colonization in the Congo because it was the bloodiest."[31]

One of the people who contributed significantly to the massive suffering of the Congolese people and the bloodshed that characterized the colonial exploitation of the Congo was the British explorer-journalist Henry Morton Stanley. While Stanley's travels made him a great celebrity in Europe and the United States, people in the Congo experienced him as a "brutal taskmaster, quick to flog his porters or to [completely destroy] any African villages that threatened to impede his progress, and, at all times, to shoot first and ask questions later."[32] The result was a trail of bodies left in his wake. When people in villages saw his caravan coming or his steamboats on the Congo River or its tributaries, they fled into the African wilderness for days without food. People who went to look for them later would only find decomposed bodies and/or bones.

As the first European to map most of the course of the Congo River, he is the one who gave detailed information about resources in the Congo to

29. Hochschild, "Introduction," viii.
30. Ibid., viii.
31. Ndaywell, *Histoire Générale du Congo, 339*.
32. Ibid., ix.

King Leopold of Belgium, after Britain seemed not interested in adding another colony to its already troubled relationships with its existing colonies. King Leopold of Belgium became the sole owner of the only private colony in the world—and he called it the Congo Free State; clearly a misnomer, given the harsh treatment and repression of the people in the colony.

From the very beginning of Leopold's colony, the foundation of the Congo Free State's economy, as in most of colonial Africa, was forced labor—and this continued well after the king's death and after the Congo became a Belgian colony in 1908. In the early years of the colony, Leopold and his agents were interested in ivory, which served some of the uses of plastic today. It also was used to make jewelry, piano keys, and false teeth.[33] But in the early 1890s, with the invention of the inflatable tire, followed by that of the automobile, a much larger source of Congo wealth developed—rubber. To maximize quick profits, the colonial regime devised a harshly effective system. The army would send a group of soldiers into a village and seize women and children as hostages. To have their wives and children released, the men were required to go into the forest to begin the scrupulous job of extracting rubber. They were given a monthly quota to fulfill. A village that refused to provide this commodity would be completely destroyed.[34]

Other forms of punishment included whipping people to death, using the *chicotte* (which was a whip made of sun-dried hippopotamus leather with razor-sharp edges; people were given a hundred lashes of the chicotte or more, with fatal consequences). Other punishments included cutting off of hands/severing of hands; cutting off of peoples' ears and noses, in order to push people to produce more rubber; and other kinds of dismemberment. So, discipline was pitiless: people who failed to gather enough rubber were punished very severely or even killed in the process. Because of this harsh treatment and sadistic punishments, the population of the Congo was slashed in half, between 1880 and 1920—some estimated 10 million people were victims of murder, starvation, exhaustion, exposure to disease, and a plummeting birth rate, as many women refused to bring children in such an unfriendly, brutal environment. Congolese historian, Isidore Ndaywel e Nziem, puts the death toll at roughly 13 million.[35] This discovery led some historians and political scientists, Western and African, to talk about the

---

33. Ibid., xii.
34. Ibid., xiv.
35. Ndaywel e Nziem, *Histoire Generale du Congo*, 344.

"forgotten holocaust" in the Congo, because the death toll was on a scale comparable to the Jewish Holocaust and Stalin's cleansings.[36]

Hochschild states that the rubber terror meant that the missionaries, for example, who had come to the Congo eager to evangelize and to impart to Africans a "Victorian sense of sin, had trouble finding bodies to clothe or souls to save." One British missionary reports being asked repeatedly by Africans, "[Does] the Savior you tell us [about] have any power to save us from rubber trouble?"[37] And there is a sense in which this question is still relevant today, given the replication and re-enactment of postcolonial violence and trauma in the Congo.

Because some missionaries engaged in religious discourse that legitimized European political and military conquest as a way to facilitate the conversion and salvation of indigenous people, they failed to adequately address this question. Others boldly spoke out against the atrocities, often at a greater danger to themselves. Others said nothing. In many ways this question has not been answered in a theologically satisfying way, given the fact that the devastating legacies of Belgian colonialism continue to affect the Congolese society and institutions. Today we can still ask whether Christianity has the power to save the Congolese from the ghosts of King Leopold and Mobutu.[38] This is still a pertinent question particularly because Congolese Christianity has tended, historically, to seek accommodation and proximity with the government and the political elites instead of taking an explicit, bold, and consistent prophetic stance against political injustices and abuses, in defense of ordinary people's rights in society.

## COLONIAL VIOLENCE AND TRAUMA PERSIST IN CONGOLESE SOCIETY

Nigerian scholar Olufemi Taiwo, writing about the profound effects of colonialism and globalization on Africa and its peoples, points out that the ghosts of colonialism continue to haunt our relations across the globe, even though we talk as if they have been slain and exorcised.[39] The works of Belgian historian Jules Marchal and American historian Adam Hochschild expand on this theme as they respectively examine ways in which the

36. Hochschild, "Introduction," xii-x.
37. Hochschild, *King Leopold's Ghost*, 172.
38. Spaas, *How Belgium Colonized*, 27–30.
39. Taiwo, *How Colonialism Preempted Modernity in Africa*, 242.

ghosts of British entrepreneur Lord Leverhulme (whose rapacious colonial exploitation of palm oil products coerced thousands of Congolese to work under brutal conditions with severe health consequences), and King Leopold (who ruled the Congo callously as his private property) as well as other countless colonizers continue to haunt Congolese life and exert ongoing significant damages on the Congolese society even today.[40]

A close examination of Congolese history reveals a shocking resemblance between colonial practices and current social, political, and economic patterns. As Hochschild suggests, there have been surprisingly consistent patterns over the centuries:

> Outsiders want some commodity the [Congolese] territory possesses. They extract the commodity, causing the death of thousands or millions of people in the process. They justify their seizure by portraying themselves as generous-hearted [or philanthropists who are bringing 'civilization' and/or aid]. A few brave souls blow the whistle and portray the exploitation that is going on. The world sometimes briefly pays attention. Then the cycle begins again with a new commodity.[41]

David Renton and his colleagues have argued that since Henry Stanley's collaboration with King Leopold in looting the country of its mineral resources, Congo's history has been one of collaboration by a minority indigenous elite with Western powers and foreign companies, and struggle by the majority against external domination and extractive exploitation of the country to the neglect and detriment of general Congolese interest and well-being.[42]

These patterns are deeply entrenched in Congolese life. Most recently, these profoundly rooted displays of violent economic extraction practices are manifested in the disputes that have resulted in a war, from 1997 to 2003, that has caused the death of more than 6 million people in what some have called one of the bloodiest conflicts since World War II. More people are continuing to die in these ongoing conflicts as they are caught between warring factions vying for access to and control of mineral resources in Eastern Congo, where local warlords and multinational corporations extract billions of dollars' worth of gold, timber, diamonds, coltan, and other minerals, with the complicity of the ruling political class concerned only

---

40. See Marchal, *Lord Leverhulme's Ghosts*, and Hochschild, *King Leopold's Ghost*.
41. Hochschild, "Introduction," in *Lord Leverhulme's Ghosts*, p.ix.
42. Renton, David, David Seddon, and Leo Zeilig, *The Congo: Plunder and Resistance*.

about filling their personal pockets and not building the country or improving the life of the Congolese people.[43] Statistics show that 80 percent of the population survives on $.30 a day and the United Nations estimates that 75 percent of the population is undernourished. In addition, there are "an estimated 1.3 million displaced Congolese, an estimated 1.1 million are living with HIV/AIDS, and close to two-thirds of the population cannot afford conventional health care."[44]

The continuing practice of extractive colonialism had maintained the colonial practice of forced labor, although the system became considerably less severe and less draconian starting in the 1920s because colonial officials realized that if they did not change their harsh colonial methods they would soon have no labor force left. People were overworked and the system could not be sustained. But the humiliating punishments for failing to comply with the demands of colonial economic extraction and forced labor itself continued until independence in 1960.

Indeed, forced labor remained a crucial part of the Belgian economy in the Congo, although it took a less murderous bent. The enforcement mechanism of taking women, children or chiefs as hostages was gradually replaced by that of taxes—and the threat of severe punishment for Congolese who did not pay them. Like in other parts of Africa, the European colonists used head taxes to *force* people away from subsistence agriculture and into mines, factories and other sectors of the colonial economy. This legacy of forced labor has remained in various forms. It is manifested in circumstances where Congolese teachers and other public workers, for example, would go several months or years without any pay; or being paid very low wages that cannot help people sustain their families adequately. Although people are not directly forced to work for free, the lack of a living wage or delayed payment of salaries are indirect forms of forced labor, which reflect the pervasive legacies of colonial abuse. These practices unnecessarily force Congolese people to live in dire conditions, while the small political and economic elite live in incredible abundance and wealth. And the simple explanation of this poverty and disparity is the corruption of the ruling political class and foreign exploitation.

---

43. DR Congo has significant quantities of coltan, a substance used in computer chips and cell phones; it is tragic that, instead of benefiting from the high global demands for this commodity, the Congolese people are dying as a result of the disputes over who extracts, sells, and distributes this highly coveted mineral.

44. Breaking the Silence on the Congo, 1.

The violence of economic extraction continued throughout the colonial period. In the 1920s, colonial officials began to construct the rudiments of a public health system and eventually what became by some assessments the continent's best networks of primary schools. Belgian industrialists and mine owners built clinics and schools because they wanted a healthy workforce and an indigenous elite class with basic education to assist the ruling colonizer class. But the roads and railways were built entirely to carry African raw materials to the ports where they could be shipped to Europe. No wonder, some historians and political scientists have characterized this as "Belgium's imperialist rape of Africa."[45]

It is also important to note that the idea of having an educated "workforce" did not include high school for all, and definitely not higher education. People were educated to serve as clerks and aides to colonial administrators and not to hold positions of leadership. At independence in 1960, for example, the country had less than five university graduates. So, there was a policy of not really educating the Congolese natives for fear that they will begin to reclaim the same rights as their European counterparts. This suspicion toward education and intellectuals is one of the continuing legacies of Belgian colonialism in the Congo. Mobutu Seseko Seko, who was dictator for thirty-two years after the assassination of Patrice Lumumba (the first elected Prime Minister, and a victim of colonial violence), maintained a Belgian colonial ideology that said, *"pas d'intellectuels, pas de problemes"* (no intellectuals, no problems). To strengthen his power, Mobutu made sure the intellectuals were silenced. And he would say in Lingala: *"soki ozali d'accord na biso te, kende epai mosusu"* (If you do not agree with us, go somewhere else). Mobutu was notorious in the way he punished his opponents. Like King Leopold of Belgium, he ordered mass killings of people who opposed him; he hanged his famous opponents publically to teach others a lesson not to attempt resisting his power. And like King Leopold, he used the Congo as his personal property as he amassed incredible wealth, while most of the people remained in abject poverty. The way Mobutu ruled is a clear example of how colonial violence was replicated and re-enacted in the Democratic Republic of Congo. As a former officer in the *Force Publique*, the army of King Leopold and later of the Belgian colonial government, he used the same methods of the colonists. There were several revolts and resistance movements against King Leopold and Mobutu, but Mobutu's response, just like Leopold's, was brutal, ruthless,

---

45. Dummett, *King Leopold's Legacy*.

and without mercy. Mobutu's case is a classic example of the transmission of postcolonial trauma, whereby an African inflicts wounds on other Africans, exactly in the ways that Europeans colonial officers did and for the same purposes: maintaining power and political domination at any cost and by any means necessary.

Indeed, King Leopold's ruthless rule has been described as the template by which Congo's rulers have governed ever since; and the method of governance they use has been described as "robbery enforced by violence."[46] Observing the current political and economic situation shows that the tendency to rule the country as a personal property is an ongoing and persistent reality. The chronic political and economic instability being currently displayed confirms the fact that Congo's tumultuous history needs to be dealt with effectively in order to stop the recurring patterns of political violence that continue to paralyze efforts to build a country that is willing and capable to provide most essential services such as clean drinking water, medical care, making available electricity to most people, education and basic infrastructure, in addition to respecting fundamental human rights and promoting a culture of social justice.

Concerning the issue of education, when the Belgians started to create schools, they had in mind the formation of an "elite" group of Congolese who would learn to imitate their white teachers and mentors and be able to serve the colonial government at a very low level and support the colonial endeavor. The educated Congolese were trained to become "civilized" so as to think and behave like their European teachers and bosses. In fact, the educational process presented the white man as a model of perfection in knowledge, behavior, manners, morals, and intelligence. To become civilized meant that the educated were able to imitate the white man. And so, the Belgians developed a whole new class of people in Belgian Congo who were the civilized or *evolués*. A significant aspect of being an *evolué* was learning to behave, think, and relate like a white person, including learning to speak French. The *evolués* firmly believed that they had attained a level of civilization, which brought them much closer to whites than to the ordinary Congolese. They felt themselves charged, in turn, to propagate this civilization to the wider population.[47] The image of white as superior was deeply entrenched in the Congolese collective mind, and the residual effects of such thinking are difficult to root out completely. This mindset

---

46. Dummett, *King Leopold's Legacy*.
47. Mianda, *Colonialism*, 145; Spaas, *How Belgium Colonized*, 55–58.

and thinking may be among the issues and dynamics that are transmitted from generation to generation. For the Congo to find its footing as a nation and build a stable state that attends to the rights and needs of all, leaders need to develop a sense of identifying with the larger population, rather than distancing themselves from the very people they are claiming to serve. The hierarchical social system inherited from colonization, because it is a transmitter of postcolonial trauma, cannot allow the political class to truly be the servant leaders needed to guide society as a whole toward interrupting and overcoming the destructive power of postcolonial trauma.

The story of a United Nations (U.N.) worker in DR Congo where he was serving as part of the U.N. peace keeping forces, provides an example of the (implied) effects of the psychological consequences of colonialism for the formerly colonized as well as for former colonizers and their descendants, in the form of postcolonial melancholia. Didier Bourguet, a 44-year-old French (white) U.N. worker was accused of raping more than 20 adolescent girls in Eastern Congo. During his trial in France in 2008, he said that he knew he had a problem; but he went on to add that *"là-bas l'esprit colonial persiste; l'omme blanc a tout ce qu'il veut"* (rough translation: "a colonial mindset still persists over there; the white man has everything he wants.")[48] As I stated earlier, the effects of colonialism do not only affect the colonized, but also the colonizers, many of whom still desire dominance and control even when they no longer have social and political pre-eminence and control in a postcolonial context. But it is important for persons in leadership and society at large to be aware of ways in which we are still maintaining and transmitting postcolonial trauma through our relationships with former colonizers and other postcolonial peoples.

## TRANSMISSION OF POSTCOLONIAL TRAUMA

The experiences described above during King Leopold's rule and during Belgian rule of the Congo, as traumatic events, did not stay in the past. They are also reflected in the Congolese contemporary society. We are learning from trauma studies, and especially Jewish Holocaust studies and research on child abuse, that trauma in its various forms (e.g., historical trauma, cultural trauma, colonial trauma, postcolonial trauma, psychological trauma) can be transmitted from generation to generation. Researchers have found that there is an ongoing trans-generational transmission of

48. Demeestere, *Un Ex-employé de l'*.

holocaust trauma in families of holocaust survivors.[49] This has led them to ask, "Why are children of Holocaust survivors still experiencing the effects of the Holocaust as if they themselves had actually been there?"[50] These same patterns have been identified among African American communities, Native American communities, as well as among other postcolonial indigenous peoples and communities.[51] Child abuse studies have also shown that the "generational cycle of abuse" occurs when maltreated children become maltreating parents.[52] Four prevalent theories of trauma transmission have been identified in the literature: 1) psychodynamic theories; 2) sociocultural theories; 3) family systems theories; and 4) biological theories. It is beyond the scope of this chapter to discuss each theory in detail; so I will present a very brief summary of what each model teaches us about the mechanisms of trauma transmission across generations, and then will briefly summarize the importance of using all these four models to gain insights into the mechanisms involved in the maintenance and transmission of postcolonial trauma. Gaining such an understanding is the first step toward healing as we will gain insights into the mechanisms of transmission and ways to identify and interrupt the transmission patterns.

1. The psychodynamic approach focuses on individual developmental history as shaped by unconscious mechanisms between parents and their children, emotions that could not be consciously experienced by the first generation are given to the second. For example, trauma that was not processed and integrated is passed on to the second generation,

---

49. Kellerman, *Transmission of Holocaust Trauma*, 1.

50. Kellerman, "*Transmission of Holocaust Trauma*, 2.

51. For discussions of postcolonial trauma in the experience of Native Americans, African Americans, and other people of color, see Betty Bastien et al, "Healing the Impact of Colonization, Genocide, and Racism on Indigenous Populations," in *The Psychological Impact of War Trauma on Civilians: An International Perspective*, ed. Stanley Krippner and Teresa M. McIntyre (Westport, Connecticut: Praeger, 2003), pp.25–37; Joy DeGruy, *Post Traumatic Slave Syndrome: America's Legacy of Enduring Injury and Healing* (Uptone Press, 2005); Sekou Mims, Larry Higginbottom, Omar Reid, *Post Traumatic Slavery Disorder* (Dorchester, MA: Pyramid Builders, Year?); Maria Yellow Horse Brave Heart and Tina Deschenie, "Historical Trauma and Post-Colonial Stress in American Indian Populations," *Tribal College Journal of American Indian Higher Education*, Vol. 17, No.3, Spring 2006, pp.24–27; Eduardo Duran, *Native American Postcolonial Psychology* (New York: State University of New York, 1995); E.J.R. David, *Filipino/American Postcolonial Psychology: Oppression, Colonial Mentality, and Decolonization* (Bloomington, IN: AuthorHouse, 2011).

52. Cerulli, et al., *Maternal Intergenerational Transmission*, 20.

whose tasks is to mourn and attempt to reverse the humiliation and feelings of helplessness that their parents experienced.[53] The transmission occurs through an unconscious process of projective identification whereby the parent carrying the trauma projects the unresolved feelings of terror, anxiety, and powerlessness into the child, and the child unconsciously interjects these feelings and experiences them as if he or she had suffered the initial trauma. As Auerhahn and Laub observe, "the massive psychic trauma shapes the internal representations of reality, becoming an unconscious organizing principle passed on by parents and internalized by their children."[54] Awareness about this transmission process can enable parents to ensure that they are not unconsciously passing on the unresolved trauma they are carrying, by developing, among other things, the capacity for self-differentiation between themselves and their children that allows them to sufficiently process and resolve their traumatic experiences.

2. The sociocultural orientation focuses on the socio-cultural aspects of the transmission, examining social learning and socialization models of transmission in terms of how the family's culture, social norms and beliefs are passed down from one generation to the next. While psychodynamic theories focus on unconscious and indirect influences, social learning theories emphasize conscious and direct effects of parents on their children. Other socializing institutions such as schools, community organizations, and religious institutions also play a significant role in this transmission process. Postcolonial trauma as cultural trauma is deeply woven into these various cultural arenas and, thus, can be transmitted from generation to generation as persons participate in these organizations. Social norms, cultural practices, beliefs, and values can be carriers of internalized colonization and oppression. An important question to ask is, what traces of traumatization patterns are reflected in these arenas, and what to do undercut their effects?

3. The family systems approach explores the formative power of patterns of communication and interactions among family members; being enmeshed with their parents, siblings and other survivors bring parents and their children into mutual identifications where parents live

---

53. Kellerman, *Transmission of Holocaust Trauma*, 7.
54. Auerhahn and Laub, *"Intergenerational Memory of the Holocaust,"* 22–23.

vicariously through their children and children live vicariously in the terrible past of their parents. Trauma is transmitted through the communication and interaction patterns as parents and children are entangled in close transactions with one another. Postcolonial trauma as a phenomenon that affects individuals, communities, and institutions can be transmitted through family dynamics and patterns of communication and interactions.[55] Clarity about how one's family is affected by cultural trauma and being intentional about functioning from a self-differentiated position can be one way to mitigate against the transmission of trauma. Self-differentiation is the capacity to define one's own life goals and values apart from togetherness forces in any emotional system such as the family, workplace, or organization. As a life-long process, self-differentiation empowers a person to maintain a non-anxious presence in the midst of one's family and other anxious groups and to take maximum responsibility for one's own destiny and emotional well-being.[56] Parents who are self-differentiated have a clear internal guiding system that enables them to self-regulate in ways that equips them to process and resolve their past trauma, without passing it on to their children. Indeed, parents who are well differentiated are able to raise well differentiated children capable of functioning from a self-differentiated position that allows them to relate more adaptively to their parents, without taking on their parents' anxiety or trauma.[57]

4. Biological models of the transmission of trauma are based on the assumption that there may be a genetic and/or biochemical predisposition to the etiology of a person's illness.[58] As Harvery suggests, there is evidence to support that some mental illness can be heredi-

---

55. See, for example, Edward Wimberly's description of the Transgenerational Family Theory and its insights into how trauma is transmitted from one generation to the next. Wimberly states that over generations, families develop patterns for responding to crises and life transitions. These patterns generate family legacies. It is in the process of responding to crises and dealing with life transitions that a parent's emotional wounds from traumatic experiences are passed on through this system. This is how a parent's traumatic wounds can inherited by successive generations. Wimberly, *Counseling African American*, 38–50.

56. Friedman, "Bowen Therapy," 141.

57. For more discussion of a family systems approach to the transmission of trauma, see Pinderhughes, "The Multigenerational Transmission."

58. Kellerman, *Transmission of Holocaust Trauma*, 11.

tary or, at least, raise the likelihood that if a parent suffers from some mental illness, their offspring has a greater chance of contracting the same illness. In this sense, holocaust trauma may be likewise passed on.[59] Kellerman recognizes that the investigation of genetic models of transmission is complicated by the fact that genes interact with environmental influences to increase or decrease susceptibility to a specific disorder. The biological models must be understood, then, from a broader and more integrative perspective that includes the psychoanalytic, family systems, and sociocultural approaches. In this sense, an integrative perspective can help us take into consideration the interplay among different levels of transgenerational influence, pointing us toward an understanding that the transmission of postcolonial trauma happens at various levels of individual, familial, and collective experience and is caused by multiple factors, including biological, individual developmental history, family influences, culture and social location.

Indeed, if we apply these four mechanisms of trauma transmission to the Congolese colonial and postcolonial situation, we can see that the unresolved complex colonial trauma was unconsciously transmitted from generation to generation as people internalized colonial oppression through the years. Descendants of traumatized people and groups unconsciously absorbed the repressed and insufficiently processed colonial trauma, thus carrying the trauma and passing it on to the next generation, including through the biological transmission process. Internalized terror, anxiety, oppression, and powerlessness were unconsciously passed on through family relationships and interactions with significant persons and close relatives and associates; these dimensions of postcolonial trauma were also carried out and transmitted through cultural practices, social norms, beliefs, and values that regulate social life and individual functioning in society. Traces of postcolonial trauma are clearly evident in Congolese life in the various dimensions noted above. But it is important to note here that this assertion is not in any way intended to pathologize the Congolese people or the country as a whole. Trauma in and of itself is not a pathology; but rather an experience that signals that something intensely violent and disorienting happened to a person or group. Trauma theory provides a radical paradigm shift in the mental health fields in that it does not locate problems

59. Harvery, *"Intergenerational Transmission of Trauma,"* 8.

within individuals; instead, it proposes that most individuals who suffer from mental and emotional distress have been injured within their social contexts. As Sandra Bloom observes, trauma theory has changed the fundamental question asked in mental health fields from "What's wrong with you?" to "What's happened to you?"[60] In the case of postcolonial trauma, there is an indication, among other things, that a profound injury or tear has happened in the social and psychic fabric of life because of intense violence and extremely repressive situations. Trauma theory helps us to recognize this reality and to explore pathways to healing and transformation.

## PATHWAYS TO HEALING AND TRANSFORMATION

The DRC is a country still reeling from the devastating effects of colonial violence and trauma. Contemporary understandings of trauma and its transmission can be very helpful in guiding and empowering Congolese people, individually and collectively, to see and understand ways in which colonialism is deeply embedded into Congolese political, social, and religious life, including the manner in which the devastating effects of colonial violence and trauma, as aspects of Congo's brutal history, are being reenacted and replicated from generation to generation. Contemporary understandings of trauma clearly can help us to see that the Congolese people were not only demoralized, abused, and dehumanized, but also deeply traumatized and, as has been noted above, continue to suffer the devastating effects of colonial violence and trauma even today. The recurrence of political instability, including the ongoing sporadic outburst of violence and armed conflicts in Eastern Congo, are the ongoing effects of postcolonial trauma.

But it is also true that the Congolese people came out of the colonial experience with strength, resiliency, and determination to resist colonialism, dictatorship, and other kinds of domination. However, because their colonial trauma has never been collectively acknowledged, consciously memorialized, sufficiently dealt with, and/or systematically addressed at the larger societal level, the losses and devastations sustained throughout the colonial and postcolonial periods have never been collectively mourned and the multigenerational transmission of postcolonial trauma patterns has never been collectively interrupted through a collective mechanism of identifying, naming, and interrupting the transmission patterns. Postcolonial trauma, as a form of internalized colonization, continues to oppress

60. Bloom, *Creating Sanctuary*.

and brutalize Congolese life. There is a need to engage in efforts to identify resources and practices for the transformation of Congolese collective consciousness in order to break with a brutal and ugly past and begin to envision a new future without the ongoing impacts of colonial violence. The past cannot be undone or repaired, but it can be used to understand the present and provide insights for the work that needs to be done for a better future, freed from the influences of a grossly traumatic past. It is such knowledge that will help transform Congolese collective consciousness.

Another resource and practice that can be transformative at both a personal and collective levels is the narrative therapy concept of *externalization*—the process of identifying the problem and separating it from oneself.[61] A major goal of narrative therapy is to alter the problem-saturated story to reflect a preferred narrative. This involves helping persons and groups to frame their problems in such a way that they can see alternatives or new avenues open to them and thus lead them to the resolution of their problem. A key assertion of narrative therapy is the belief that people should not be equated with their problems. People *have* problems; they are *not* problems.[62] In other words, problems are not major identifying features for persons. Hence, the key practice of externalizing problems is intended to free individuals and groups from the bondage of constricting stories they tell about themselves so they can envision a new identity and create alternative ways of looking at themselves and their potentials.

Given the dynamics of postcolonial trauma as internalized colonization and oppression, externalization can help support efforts to identify internalized colonization and oppression as problems to struggle against, rather than issues inherent in individual or collective identity and self-understanding. The process of externalization is particularly helpful for people who experience severe colonial violence because they tend to internalize their oppressive experience as a part of them. As a result, they can develop distorted images of the world and of themselves, including becoming themselves carriers and transmitters of the violence they have suffered. The reenactment of violence seems inevitable since the internalized oppression has become a part of them. However, the colonized people can be helped to externalize the problem and begin to see their postcolonial trauma experience as something caused by forces outside of themselves (i.e., as something done *to* them), and in that sense they could then begin to create new narratives that are freed from

---

61. Morgan, *What Is Narrative Therapy?* 17.
62. Nichols, *Family Therapy*, 350–351.

negative influences rooted in colonial trauma. Trauma theory and narrative therapy can be very useful resources in helping the Congolese people develop awareness of the sources of the recurring political violence and social instability as issues not internal to the Congolese people's identity, but rather as problems caused by specific political and cultural practices and values deeply rooted in the colonial experience of trauma. More specifically, internalized colonization and oppression are the sources of the recurring political violence and social distress.

Indeed, political violence and social instability have been constant features of life in the Congo. There has never been a nonviolent transition of power in the country since it gained independence from Belgium in 1960. In fact, political violence and social and economic instability, including instability of political institutions, have been recurring marks of Congolese life. There is a need to develop societal behaviors, attitudes, and patterns, including the development of leadership styles that do not carry and/or transmit colonial trauma. Liberation from the influences of colonial violence and trauma could lead to a beautiful remaking of the Congolese nation's relationship with its violent colonial and postcolonial history and thus lead to the creation of preferred new narratives and empowering pathways to a more dignified and peaceful future. Indeed, to be able to do all these things, there is a need to develop a collective historical consciousness that creates a passion to know and learn the lessons of the brutal and ugly colonial history in order to overcome internalized colonization and oppression and to begin to externalize these dynamics as intrusions that diminish well-being and human flourishing. Doing all this will be the beginning of the healing process.

# Chapter 6

## The Aftermath of Violence
*A SECURE Pastoral Care Model of Healing and Wholeness*

### Mazvita Machinga Ph.D.
Pastoral Psychotherapist, Zimbabwe

IN THIS CHAPTER, I describe a personal journey with survivors of political violence in Zimbabwe. Between 2000 and 2008 Zimbabweans went through a wave of politically motivated violence. Thousands of people had their homes and property burned and their loved ones murdered and forcibly evicted from their homes. During these years, there was immense suffering, communities disintegrated, and lives were shattered. In such cases, and after the wave of violence, survivors of politically motivated and sexual violence were expected to heal while still living in the presence of their perpetrators. This made their suffering vivid, painful, and it complicated the healing process. A glance through today's media, chances are you will find more stories on emotional, spiritual, physical, and psychological breakdown emanating from violent encounters of some sort, be it political violence, domestic violence, sexual violence, and/or community violence. Within families, communities, and churches there are scores of people encountering violence in one way or the other. What is painful is that, according to Judith Herman, the ordinary response to most of these atrocities is to banish them from consciousness.[1] Unfortunately, in these experiences, an attempt is done to neglect aspects of healing and reconciliation and these painful experiences continue to haunt and trouble survivors. In the aftermath of violence, people are left trying to make sense of their lives and build a way forward.[2] Hence, the purpose of this chapter is to discuss and highlight interventions that have assisted victims as they move forward towards healing and recovery after encountering violence. Even though the focus is on political violence, the interventions discussed have been found to apply to any form of healing and reconciliation after encountering violence.

Additionally, in this chapter I discuss effective care interventions that assist survivors as they get back on their feet and make a positive way forward in their lives. The chapter is informed by the multiple realities and subjective meanings of research participants who I interviewed during my Ph. D dissertation. In this chapter, I review my experience in the interviewing and the counseling of primary and secondary survivors of politically motivated violence. I also review how different experiences with exposure to political violence shape human behavior and self-concept. In addition, I also highlight some clustered critical aspects that surround the psychological, emotional, social, and spiritual survivors experiences with violence. I conclude by outlining helpful and meaningful interventions that emerged from the discussions with the research participants, which states the importance of integrating spiritual and mental health care in a community response framework to trauma. I present in this chapter an intervention model, namely, The SECURE model. The model strives to attain **S**urvivor **E**mpowerment through **C**aring, **U**nderstanding, **R**estoration of human dignity, and **E**fforts to meet their survival needs. The SECURE model effectively facilitates healing and reconciliation in the aftermath of violence in an African context. I argue that for effective healing and reconciliation to happen, a model, which is three prong such as SECURE, works better in that it attends to the victim's reality, listens to what drives the perpetrators' behavior, while also strengthening the capacity of communities in addressing the visible and invisible wounds caused by exposure to violence. Even though the information was gathered from Zimbabwean survivors of political violence, findings apply to various situations of violence. Consideration of issues will enable service providers, caregivers, communities,

---

1. Herman, *Trauma*, 1.
2. Lederach,and Lederach, *When Blood and Bones*, 7.

and churches to understand the impact of violence on human well-being while embracing interventions that will inspire communities to engage in transformational healing and reconciliation.

## SURVIVORS' EXPERIENCES OF VIOLENCE

As I write this chapter, I reflect on the survivors and perpetrators' stories, which I heard during my interviews. It was a humbling experience for me, in some instances, to be the only witness to the survivors' stories. Some of them had not had any opportunity to share their pains, fears, and struggles with anyone. This is because the encounter of injuring and threatening to self or others involve the experience of intense fear, helplessness, or horror.[3] As I listened to the survivors' stories, I wrote down the spiritual, theological, and psychological needs that emerged from their accounts. I also listed the various issues they mentioned as helpful to them. Survivors are hurt in many ways. As asserted by Darlene Fuller Rogers, a theologian, "all forms of trauma—physical and psychological—have an effect on one's spirituality."[4] Jonas, one of the research participants, shares similar thoughts. He said, "Political violence caused lots of damages, people were hurt spiritually, relationships were ruined, some people's businesses were destroyed, all this means that there is need for healing, the need is there."[5] I also noticed that several issues that the survivors talked about seemed to cluster in certain patterns and in various levels. As asserted by John Paul Lederach and Angela Jill Lederach in their statement, "violence displaces people at multiple levels, fracturing their sense of safety in the world."[6] Most survivors felt displaced emotionally, psychologically, spiritually, and sometimes communally, too. I learned about the need for deliberate healing and reconciliation programs to assist survivors as they forged on with life. It was clear and loud from the survivors' narratives that if the pain, fear, anger, and grief are not given appropriate care, understanding, and attention, their feelings, thoughts, and behaviors are negatively impacted. From my interviews, I noticed how the survivors' experiences were clustered in critical aspects, namely, the need to be heard, the need to reconnect with self and others, the need to be empowered and restored, and the need to

3. Criterion A of the Diagnostic and Statistical Manual of Mental Disorders
4. Rogers and Fuller, *Pastoral Care for Post-Traumatic Stress Disorder*, 8.
5. Jonas Interview by Machinga.
6. Lederach and Lederach, *When Blood and Bones Cry Out*, 7.

integrate the experience in a way that helps them move on with life. Survivors and perpetrators needed to be SECURE as they faced their future. A sense of inner and outer security was imperative for moving on with life. The following are highlights of some clustered, critical aspects from the survivors' experiences.

a. *The need to be heard*

After encountering violence many survivors' past hurts and loss stories needed attention and validation. Most survivors' painful experiences remained secret, as asserted by one of the survivors when he said, "In my community I have not heard of anyone telling their experiences, people are not free to share about their experiences because we are not quite sure of what will happen after that. There is no confidence of protection. Intimidation is still around in some areas."[7] Just because it is not easy for survivors to have someone hear their stories, they remain fixated in the pain. Even after many months and years, the survivors needed to talk, the memories continued to sting them periodically. From the interviews I could see that most of the time survivors were typically preoccupied with the nature of the injuries inflicted on them, the brutality of the violent acts, the types of weapons used, and the suffering they encountered, either witnessing it or directly experiencing the violence. Some survivors had to grapple with the reality of staying with dead relatives at home on their own without any one being there to quickly assist. Even though this was so, the hidden rule was 'do not say, do not feel.' Such a situation leads to high levels of distress, where an environment to speak out on what was done to them and how that impacted their lives would go a long way in soothing the survivors. They need to do so without fear of further victimization or stigmatization. Being heard means that they are able to vent their emotions and start to move on with life. Noah Cannon affirms the dangers of not acknowledging or paying attention to survivors' experiences by saying, "when survivors' needs are neglected, misunderstood, or denied by others or by one self, harm to all people concerned may result."[8] As a result of suppression of emotions and experiences, survivors in particular were affected. Some of them reported common psychological discomfort such as not sleeping well, increased anxiety and sadness,

---

7. Interview by Machinga.
8. Cannon, *Roots of Violence*, 57.

feeling of hostility, and losing focus and concentration during day-to-day functioning. They also reported having unexplainable physiological discomfort such as loss of appetite, insomnia, and general fatigue. This means that the survivors reacted to traumatic cues and reminders with disturbing somatic symptoms and uncharacteristic deterioration in behavior. Not only will talking about experiences help them to vent, it also help survivors share their distress so that they can be directed to appropriate help. "Any symptoms they experience will be explained, normalized, demystified, depathologized, and validated. As a result of the sharing their stories, pertinent interventions such as relaxation, desensitization, and other effective cognitive-behavioral or psycho-physiological techniques will be explored and communicated."[9] Where possible, opportunities should be given to explore spiritual practices that help survivors take back some control of their lives. Successful healing and reconciliation happens when survivors' experiences are validated and their strengths supported. So, it is important to provide a gentle environment where survivors talk about their emotions, pain, and their needs.

b. *The need to restore relationship and reconnect with self and others*

All the participants reported that relationships in families and communities have been broken. People continue to have bitter feelings toward each other. According to the participants, some perpetrators do not show any remorse for the harm they caused on other people. Exposure to political violence, and any other form of violence, makes survivors lose important beliefs about themselves and the world around them. As asserted by Miller Laurence, "The most distressing aspect of their fundamental beliefs about themselves, the world, and the other people that had previously shaped their lives."[10] So, knowing that recovery from violence can only take place within the context of relationships, it cannot occur in isolation, it is crucial that survivors have an opportunity to reconnect. This is affirmed by Herman when she says:

> In renewed connections with other people, the survivor re-creates the psychological faculties that were damaged or deformed by the traumatic experiences. These faculties include basic capacities for trust, autonomy initiative, competence, identity and intimacy. Just

9. Miller, *Psychological Inteventions*, 283–296.
10. Ibid., 283–296.

as these capabilities are originally formed in relationships with other people, they must be reformed in such relationships.[11]

This need for reconnection is echoed by one of the survivors when he said, "If victims and perpetrators learn to interact, see each other as kins, then go on as usual, relationships could be brought back to their original place. [Then] I think we will be alright."[12] This survivor was bringing out the importance of reconnecting and the restoring of relationships in post-violence situations. This is what Lederach and Lederach term social healing. In fact, one-hundred-percent of the survivors that I interviewed acknowledged that the healing of interpersonal relations in communities that have been greatly hurt by violence and conflict is vital for realizing genuine social healing. Therefore, there is great need for rebuilding and mending of relations if healing and reconciliation are to take place. Since social healing has to do with mending broken relationships, rebuilding trust, and restoration of hope, it is the healing that most survivors wish for. In collectivistic traditional societies, like Zimbabwe, social healing is a form of healing that survivors feel as central if communities are to re-build their communities. The disintegration of the communal relations is a blow to the societal fabric of people, as all the interviews echoed. They view community as a vessel that safely holds people during times of crisis. James O'Dea and Judith Thompson of the Institute of Noetic Sciences acknowledge the role of social healing by saying, "many now believe that to truly heal the greater social body requires addressing the healing needs of individuals and the transformation of social institutions concurrently. Truth, justice, compassion, and peace all appear to be necessary elements in social healing."[13] What O'Dea and Thompson are saying is that individuals and communities are able to re-build trust and restore hope when social healing is realized. Even more important, as O'Dea cited in Lederach and Lederach, "Social healing seeks to deal with the wounds created by conflict, collective trauma, and large-scale oppression."[14] From this quote, healing of social wounds takes into account all dimensions from the personal to the political. Social healing

11. Herman, *Trauma and Recovery*, 133.
12. Chigere Interview by Machinga.
13. O'Dea and Thompson, *Social Healing*.
14. Lederach and Lederach, *When Blood and Bones*, 7.

"brings to a culture of violence seeds of new possibilities," says O'Dea and Thompson. This is done through the honoring and valuing of human life and relationships.[15] Herman also emphasized the need for reconnection when she says, t"[that] reconnection is a core experience in recovery. As survivors reconnect, they feel calmer and better able to face life with equanimity.[16] When survivors reconnect, they are likely to share their needs and relevant interventions are implemented. Once people have acquired social healing, they have reconnected and have a sense of belonging and of being valued and they become empowered with hope, and are renewed and ready to move on. This brings me to the next important need of survivors if authentic healing is to take place.

c. *The need to be empowered, renew hope and move on with life*

Research participants shared that many healing interventions are needed to empower and equip survivors with coping skills and also with livelihood skills. Survivors who are empowered are better able to confront the negative effects of political violence. From the survivors' stories, it was clear that disempowerment and disconnection are core experiences of psychological trauma. As stated by Herman, "recovery, therefore, is based upon the empowerment of the survivor and the recreation of important relationships.[17] Speaking on importance of empowerment, Jonasi said, "As a church, what I find helpful is bringing the survivors together and facilitating discussions on coping skills, where they learn what is helpful for them to heal and move on. As churches, we have a role to play in educating survivors, providing skills for the good of the society."[18] What sort of empowerment was Jonasi talking about? Survivors in post-political violence will have suffered various losses, dignity, worth, and loss of important relationships. They may also have lost their health through physical injury. They want to heal from dehumanization and many other forms of human atrocities. Borrowing some of Andrew Lester's terminology, the survivors' coping stories have will been attacked, and, thus, become "dysfunctional

---

15. O'Dea and Thompson, *"Social Healing."*
16. Herman, *Trauma and Recovery*, 203.
17. Ibid., 133.
18. Jonasi Interview by Machinga.

future stories."[19] Hence, survivors need to heal from the attacks done to their future stories. Empowering survivors helps them redirect their energies in positive ways. Implementing empowering activities with survivors of violence will come by finding ways to give power to those disenfranchised so that they can resist oppression on their own and take authority over their own lives. For the survivors that interviewed, the empowerment in post-violence Manicaland is helping them find ways to overcome effects of political violence and handling hurts.[20] Survivors need to be empowered by equipping them with positive coping skills, self-confidence, assertiveness, and livelihood skills they need to be assertive enough to say their needs, explaining what justice means to them, and making sure that justice is done. In many cases, restorative justice brings genuine healing on both victims and perpetrators. This is so because with restorative justice we focus on repairing the harm caused by atrocities. There is room for transformation, if the victims, offenders, and community members at large decide how reparations have to be done and not just give a cold shoulder to victims' experiences. With some of them having had their animals and granaries destroyed, they need to restart making a living. Perpetrators need to be empowered, too. They need to be liberated from guilt and shame if they are to integrate wholly into society. They need to acquire tools and right attitudes to make things right with the victims that they harmed. They need to gain skills of addressing self-condemnation and reintegration into community. Perpetrators need to take responsibility for their behavior. From the focus groups and the interviews with survivors, I found that forgiveness and reconciliation was most likely going to take place if perpetrators are held accountable of their actions and dialogue is facilitated between these two parties. Once this empowerment has been done, survivors regain strength, and hope is renewed so they can move on.

## HOPE

I cannot complete this section without highlighting the importance of hope in healing and reconciliation. Survivors stated that they needed

19. Lester, *Hope in Pastoral Care*, 126.
20. Watkins, *Survival and Liberation*, 139.

interventions that revive a sense of community, enlivens hopefulness, and encourages lament. A pattern during the interviews was the prevalence of the survivors' loss of finite hope in the local authorities and in the Zimbabwean government. They felt that the fragile situation in the country had taken from them the gift of being valuable citizens. They stated that the government of Zimbabwe has betrayed them, rather than being a source of support and security as portrayed in one survivors' words, "we have not seen any healing program by the government. It has taken too long a time to stop the violence in communities. The government is not doing much. The perpetrators are free to do what they want in the name of politics. Our only hope is in God, not in what is happening at the moment."[21] Most survivors had expected that the government was going to protect them instead of watching idly and doing nothing. The survivors found themselves, as portrayed in Charles Gerkin's words, "caught between a hermeneutic of despair and a hermeneutic of hope and expectation.[22] For instance, for some whose homes were destroyed during the political violence, conceptualizing what the future without a home would look like has been a nightmare. "Paradoxically, they live as neighbors and, yet, are locked into longstanding cycles of hostile interaction. The situation is characterized by deep-rooted, intense animosity, fear and severe stereotyping."[23] This is truly a picture of hope lost, thereby calling for a theology of rebuilding. I asked the survivors what was keeping them going if they had lost hope with the government and with their communities. Most of the survivors responded that their only hope has been in trusting God. Their hope has been the trust that God's purposes will prevail one day and their communities will live as one family again. Unlike Capps' perception of hope that is fueled by desire, most survivors' hope has been fueled by dependence on transcendental powers. Thus, while most survivors felt hopeless with the government, they felt hopeful in supernatural and Divine interventions.

While there has been a breakdown of hope in the government there has been strengthening of hope in God's intervention. "This situation in Zimbabwe needs God's intervention for it is only God who can bring all this suffering to an end."[24] While this may sound like a sense of giving up, there is a sense that where human power fails God succeeds. Thus, survi-

21. Toraga Interview by Machinga.
22. Lester, *Hope in Pastoral Care*, 43.
23. Lederach, *Building Peace*, 23.
24. Zinwe Interview by Machinga.

vors searched for *Dunamis* (the power of God) to sustain them. What is important is that the survivors' hope in God was the one sustaining them.

Finally, it is important to note that while the above factors realistically capture the experiences of the survivors that I interviewed, and are issues that really matter, they are non-exhaustive of the survivors' experiences. While the information above describes the survivors' experiences, healing and reconciliation has not fully been realized. The perpetrators lack accountability for the harm they did to people, making it difficult for the victims of political violence to rebuild their shattered lives. The widespread impunity of powers has empowered perpetrators to continue with violation of ordinary people's rights. Below is an outline of the various ways that the interviewed survivors saw as helpful if they were to heal from the effects of political violence.

## HELPFUL AND MEANINGFUL INTERVENTIONS THAT EMERGED FROM THE RESEARCH

From a traditional African perspective, for holistic recovery and healing to take place interventions should acknowledge the survivor experiences as mentioned above. Care interventions should also be culturally sensitive and should recognize the cultural identity of survivors. Cultural identity includes embracing transpersonal perspectives and the African spirituality. Masiiwa Reggies Gunda, a Zimbabwean scholar, affirms this recognition by saying, "For the traditional Shona there is a dual worldview—the world of the living and world of the spirits. The world of the spirits is not seen as geographically removed from the living world, rather, it permeates the world of the living. This is seen from the Shona phrase relating to the world of the spirits."[25] In addition, John Mbiti, an African theologian, affirms this point in his book, *African Religions and Philosophy*, by saying, "religion permeates into all the departments of life so fully that it is not easy or possible always to isolate it."[26] In other words, when facilitating recovery and healing interventions in the aftermath of exposure to political violence for indigenous African people, the practices should be located in the context of personal and transpersonal experiences. This means that not only should focus be on personal, physical, social, and psychological issues but focus should also be placed on the role of transpersonal realities in enabling heal-

25. Gunda, "Christianity, Traditional Religion and Healing," 2–11.
26. Mbiti, *African Religions and Philosophy*, 1.

ing and reconciliation. Care interventions must involve working with the whole and within a larger context of spiritual experience unfolding. When working with survivors in Zimbabwe, caring efforts should go beyond the traditional therapeutic approaches extending to the profound spiritual realities, which survivors need to confront. From the survivors' narration of what helps, I propose a caring model that enables restoration and healing in post-violence—the SECURE Model. This model is a pastoral care model, which enables survivors to have a secure sense of connection, empowerment, and hope.

## THE SECURE MODEL

People need internal and external security for wholesome living and stability. This can be achieved through a pastoral care model-SECURE. This pastoral care model strives to attain Survivor Empowerment through Caring, Understanding, Restoration of human dignity, and Effort to meet survivors' needs. From the experiences of the survivors that I interviewed, the SECURE model effectively facilitates healing and reconciliation in the aftermath of violence in an African context. A model, which is three-prong such as the SECURE model, works effectively in that through the model caregivers attend to the survivor's reality, listen to what drives the perpetrators' behavior, while also strengthening the capacity of communities in addressing the visible and invisible wounds caused by exposure to violence. The model involves equipping and resourcing survivors to cope with the aftereffects of political violence.

### Survivor Empowerment through Caring and Understanding

The survivors who I interviewed stated that they needed the kind of help that empowers them to confront the challenges brought about by being exposed to violence. This confrontation has to be done with honesty, hope, and faith. As shared by most research participants, it is through hope and the presence of a caring community that survivors transcend painful situations and get be back to their feet. From the survivors' input it is clear that an effective intervention is one that is caring, understanding, and able to foster healing and growth. It is one that should allow authentic expression of spirituality, truthful uncovering of events, expression of justice, remorse, and forgiveness. Post-violence healing can be achieved through understanding and caring. The diagram below shows a three-prong pastoral care model. The secure pastoral care model encompasses spiritual care, pastoral counseling, and ecclesiastical care. It is important to note that the three components of pastoral care shown in the diagram below are distinguishable but not separate. Each of the aspects contributes to the whole when it comes to restoration of wholeness and vitality. The three elements ensure safety, protection, and support for survivors. The diagram below shows the three-fold pastoral care model:

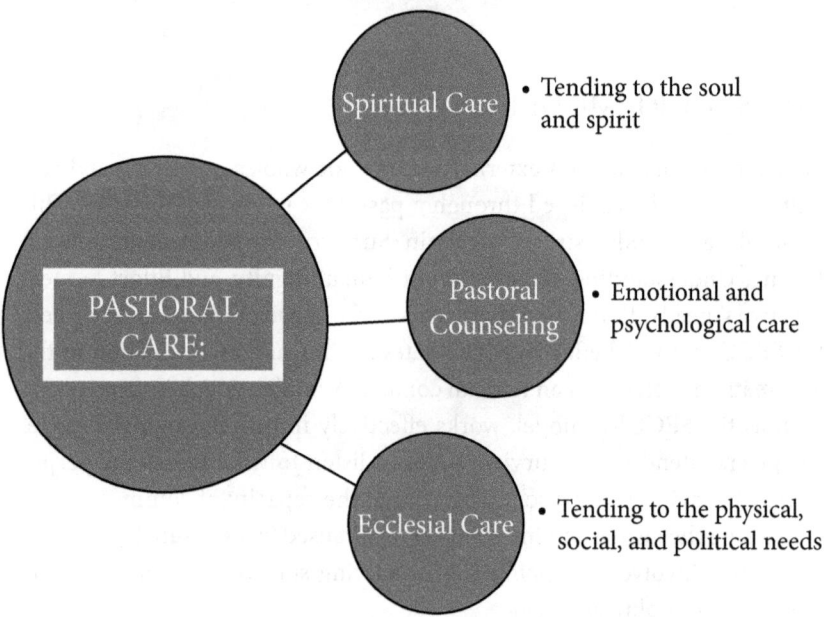

Diagram 1: The Three Components of Pastoral Care Needed in Post-Conflict Situations

From the diagram above, healing comes when the physical, spiritual, psychological, and socio-cultural aspects of survivors' experiences are addressed. In post-political violence, there is no single healing and reconciliation process, but what is needed is action, engagement, and a blend of the above caring practices. What I learned from the interviews is that as caregivers walk alongside the survivors, as supportive, caring, and understanding response mitigates the impact of violence. As asserted by Earl Shelp, "Through human presence, God becomes present and active in the world. In this SECURE model, pastoral care can be a sign that a person's suffering does not separate that person from God or from God's community of care and concern."[27] Spiritual care as one component of pastoral care includes nurturing of the human soul, connection to the Divine, and to the other. In the traditional Shona culture, spiritual care includes the solace one gets from the family elders, traditional leaders, ancestral spirits, religious traditions, or nature. In this research, spiritual care as an aspect of pastoral care is important because most survivors cope with and understand their suffering through their spiritual beliefs or the spiritual dimension of their lives.[28] In Zimbabwe, both religious and traditional believers tap into their spiritual resources when faced with life crises. The spiritual care is offered, not only by the religious representatives, but it is also offered by the community as a whole. By acknowledging the place of spirituality, survivors can begin to regain hope, trust, and faith. Survivors need to deal with existential issues that come as a result of grief, segregation, pain, and dehumanization. Attending to survivor spiritual issues helps them reclaim their identity, and realize healing of visible and invisible wounds.

Ecclesial care is a component of pastoral care that is provided through the community or religious institutions after identifying the survival and livelihood needs of victims and then exploring ways of addressing the needs. Ecclesial care is the *"hands-on concrete care"* that congregations provide to survivors. Ecclesial care comes in diverse ways that address the concrete needs of survivors. It involves assembling resources together so as to hold each other in times of crisis. Similar to Edward Wimberly's views on Pastoral Care and Black Churches, "pastoral care has to do with mobilizing the resources of the total community in caring for the needs of individuals."[29] Through ecclesial care, personhood is linked to community; hence, pastoral care that springs from the perspective of the communal care is effective. Ecclesial care emphasizes relating to one another and a sense of belonging. Its function is similar to the concept of Ubuntu. The Ubuntu African principle, which refers to *"muntu ungumuntu ngabantu"* is translated as "a person is a person through other people."[30] John Mbiti acknowledges the Ubuntu/Unhu principle by stating its significance to African people. He states that Ubuntu means, "I am because you are. You

---

27. Shelp, *"Pastoral Care as a Community Endeavour."*

28. Galek, et.al, *"Spiritual Needs."* 1–2.

29. Wimberly, *Pastoral Care in the Black Church*, 34.

30. This expression derives from local vernacular languages mostly used in the Southern part of Africa. Kasambala, *"The Impact of an African Spirituality,"* 305.

are because I am."[31] Thus, being part of community is a basic identity of being African and it serves as a safety net during moments of need. For the Shona people, healing comes through ecclesial care in relation to the other because personal is also communal. In addition, as asserted by Herman, "In the aftermath of traumatic life events, survivors are highly vulnerable. Their sense of self has been shattered. That sense can be rebuilt only as it was built initially, in connection with others."[32] So for example, churches should deliberately reach out to survivors, identifying and addressing individuals or community's humanitarian needs such as food, medication, shelter, cohesion, education, and clothing. Through various ecclesial care interventions, human suffering is lessened, hope is fostered, and holistic well-being is promoted.

The pastoral counseling part of this model is very important. This is an intervention that enables survivors to have a safe space to talk about their feelings, emotions, and needs. This is when victims lament. Survivors need support as they mourn their losses. Failure to engage in the complete normal process of grieving compromises healing and just perpetuates negative traumatic responses. Through a counseling process, survivors lament theloss of dreams, possibilities, dignity, loved ones, and property. For any healing and reconciliation process, lament is vital. Lament is about naming one's grief and sorrow in order to come to terms with reality. According to Nancy Duff, lament is important because it is "an avenue for expressing intense feelings of grief such as sorrow, complaints, and anger. Whether that grief arises from illnesses or tragedy or an act of injustice toward the worshipper, it is expressed before God and other members of the community."[33] What this means is that through pastoral counseling, survivors incorporate their losses and trauma into their lives and make it part of their identity. In pastoral counseling, lament prayers become an outlet to voice the anguish that comes from the effects of political violence. The lamentations as reported by the interviewees can be in the form of spiritual practices, rituals, liturgies, and prayers that strengthen survivors. Through lamentations, survivors have the opportunity to let go of the weight of pain and take their burden to God. In that way they feel someone is in charge of their situation. The greatest benefit of lament is enabling survivors to rely on God and have a chance to express frustrations and anger. Lament does not mean that the

---

31. Mbiti, *African Religions and Philosophy*, 61.
32. Herman, *Trauma and Recovery*, 61.
33. Duff, "*Recovering Lamentation.*" 3–14.

survivors are weak and unforgiving. It is, however, sad that most survivors that I interviewed did not have that opportunity to lament. The environment was very intimidating, such that survivors were silent. There was fear of the politicians and militia. Survivors were left with no option except to minimize what had happened to them and remained silent.

## CONCLUSION

In conclusion, in this chapter I have identified and reflected on the stories of political violence victims and the perpetrators, which I heard during doctoral program interviews. I highlighted effective care interventions that assist survivors to get back to their feet and make a positive way forward in their lives. From the survivors' experiences, I learned that there are critical clustered aspects that surround the psychological, emotional, social, and spiritual survivors' experiences with violence. I have also outlined helpful and meaningful interventions that emerged from the interviews, which states the importance of integrating spiritual and mental health care in a community response framework to trauma. I end the chapter by presenting an intervention model namely, The SECURE model. The model strives to attain Survivor Empowerment through Caring, Understanding, Restoration of human dignity, and Effort to meet their survival needs through spiritual care, pastoral counseling, and ecclesial care. I argue that for effective healing and reconciliation to happen, a model which is three-pronged, such as SECURE, works better in that it attends to the victim's reality, listens to what drives the perpetrators' behavior, while also strengthening the capacity of communities in addressing the visible and invisible wounds caused by exposure to violence. By implementing the SECURE pastoral care model, caregivers allow survivors to rebuild their once shattered lives. Without rebuilding, healing and reconciliation is difficult to attain. In an environment where considerable destruction has been done, not only to the material life of humanity, but also to the personhood of individuals, the ability to re-build becomes an opportunity to restore meaning to life and bring communities to functional wholeness. Thus, I urge all caregivers to implement the SECURE pastoral care model when reaching out to survivors of violence.

# Chapter 7

## Deliverance and Delivery
*Total Care for the Distressed, Oppressed, and Possessed*

### EMMANUEL Y. AMUGI LARTEY
CANDLER SCHOOL OF THEOLOGY, EMORY UNIVERSITY

IN CHRISTIAN CIRCLES TODAY, and especially across the African continent, practices of ministry described as 'deliverance' popularized mostly by Pentecostal and charismatic revivalists, are widespread. Drawing inspiration from the New Testament accounts of the ministry of Jesus with people described as 'possessed by demons,' Christian history records rites of exorcism performed by clergy to set people and places free from evil influences. Contemporaneously the term "deliverance ministry" is used to describe religious acts performed to free persons or places from oppression or possession by a malign or disturbing influence believed to be spiritual in nature.[1] Deliverance ministries engage in procedures, programs, or acts of spiritual intervention designed to remove from people and places troubling beings believed to be overwhelming or overcoming them through occupying their bodies, minds, spirits, inner worlds, or else external spaces. Under what could be categorized as a medical model, these ministries diagnose mental or physical illness, or distress, as being caused by identifiable spiritual entities, which, like germs, take residence within a person's body and wreak

---

1. Cook, ed., *Spirituality*, 75.

havoc upon the person's health by their nefarious activities. Their diagnosis of the causative factors, particularly in mental illness, is typically that it is due to the presence of an evil spirit or demon. Their prescribed remedy is the introduction of a spiritual intervention–such as prayer, command, or declaration–to dislodge the spirit and remove it from its place within the troubled person. Such powerful spiritual intervention is believed to be the means by which troubling spirits can be removed and, thus, mental illness cured. The cause of the illness having been taken away, the ill person is, thus, 'delivered' or set free.

In Africa, given the widespread traditional beliefs in spirits and spiritual causation of misfortune, deliverance practices have gained such a following as to frequently be an unquestioned feature of all ministry, especially that of healing and health in their broadest senses. Studies indicate that, though infrequent, belief in demonic possession and the practices of deliverance are not uncommon across the globe.[2] African churches of all persuasions these days engage in healing and deliverance services in response to the felt needs of parishioners. The outcomes of deliverance ministries have, however, frequently proved questionable, inconclusive, and at times not only unsuccessful but also harmful. Moreover, there are regularly reports in the African media, as well as concerning African immigrants in Europe and infamously recently in Britain, where physical abuse, beatings, and neglect have been meted out to children in the service of 'delivering them from evil spirits.'

## THE BIBLE AND DELIVERANCE

It is important to observe that the application of the term 'deliverance' to acts of exorcism represents a narrowing of the biblical usage. In the Bible the term deliverance applies to a much broader range of activities engaged in by God for God's people. Issues of social justice, communal well-being, political emancipation, economic empowerment, as well as personal healing are intertwined in the deliverance spoken of in the Bible. In the Old Testament, God's paradigmatic act of deliverance was the Exodus in which God acted decisively to deliver God's Hebrew people from slavery in Egypt and to bring them into a land of promise. In the New Testament, Jesus announces his public ministry through reading a portion of the book of

2. See for example, Bull, *A Phenomenological Model,* 131–139, which includes a brief historical and literary account of exorcism.

Isaiah (61:1–2) and pointing out its fulfillment through his presence and ministry:

> The Spirit of the Lord God is upon me, because he has anointed me to bring good news to the poor. He has sent me to proclaim release to the captives and recovery of sight to the blind, to let the oppressed go free, to proclaim the year of the Lord's favor (Luke 4:18–19 NRSV).

Deliverance in the Bible always tends to have a holistic and communal sense about it with total well-being for the whole people of God being its aim. The life, death, and resurrection of Jesus in the New Testament constitute God's act of deliverance for all who believe from slavery to sin into the freedom of the children of God. Those who believe in Jesus are delivered from bondage and formed into a people who together represent God's new creation.

The worldview and medical knowledge in Jesus' times are clearly distinct from that of the modern, and indeed postmodern, postcolonial world. Very real differences exist between the way people in the first century understood illness, especially mental illness and the way we do today. Nevertheless, understandings of evil and the "powers of darkness" continue to hold sway in this current era. Some interpreters of biblical material adopt a more literalistic view in which what Jesus is seen to be doing in exorcism is to be applied to the current situation without any difference.[3] Others, equally determined to be respectful to Scripture and convinced that there is something profoundly true to be learnt from the practices of Jesus, seek a more symbolic view in applying the texts to the contemporary situation.[4] Generally, those who take a more phenomenological approach to the texts take them to be about actual spiritual beings (evil angels, demons) who are able to inhabit (possess) individuals, oppress them, or harass them with illnesses or misfortunes of various kinds. Those who adopt a more symbolic approach see the biblical references as pointing to the presence and reality of evil powers and principalities, especially of a political or economic nature, or else of mental or ego states that are negative or unhealthy. The action of Jesus in expelling demons sets victims free from political domination, economic exploitation, physical illnesses of different sorts, or troubling or distressing mental states.

---

3. Basham, *Deliver Us From Evil*.
4. Walter, *Violence and Nonviolence*.

## HEALING AND DELIVERANCE IN AFRICAN CHRISTIANITY

Kwabena Asamoah-Gyadu, in a thoughtful and carefully researched study, has given us much useful insight into the beliefs, practices, and experiences of African Charismatics in relation to healing and deliverance.[5] Asamoah-Gyadu defines healing and deliverance in Ghanaian neo-Pentecostalism in the following way:

> "The deployment of divine resources, that is, power and authority in the Name or Blood of Jesus–perceived in pneumatological terms as the intervention of the Holy Spirit–to provide release for demon-possessed, demon-oppressed, broken, disturbed, and troubled persons, in order that victims may be restored to 'proper functioning order,' that is, to 'health and wholeness;' and, being, thus, freed from demonic influence and curses, they may enjoy God's fullness of life understood to be available in Christ."[6]

Asamoah-Gyadu correctly argues that "healing and deliverance," typically seen as belonging together, is utilized as a form of pastoral care aimed at restoring disturbed persons to proper functioning order again. The African Pentecostal belief ties in a causal relationship to sin, the work of demons, and sickness. Deliverance, thus, is seen as much more than exorcism (the expulsion of evil spirits). Deliverance is about freeing people from bondage to sin, Satan, and sickness.

In this regard, an important distinction is made between *possession* and *oppression*. Among the practitioners of the healing and deliverance ministries in Africa, possession has to do with "altered states of consciousness, conditions in which suffering or 'unnatural behavior' is deemed to be the result of an invasion of the human body by an alien spirit."[7] Oppression, in contrast, refers to "suffering or frustrations in life, including insomnia, poor financial management, frequent illness, failure to receive business contracts, or even lack of academic progress, all of which may be interpreted as resulting from satanic or demonic activity."[8] The oppressed may not necessarily be possessed, although oppression and possession may occur simultaneously in a person.

---

5. Asamoah-Gyadu, *African Charismatics*, 164.
6. Ibid., 165.
7. Ibid., 167
8. Ibid., 168.

## DISSOCIATIVE IDENTITY DISORDER AND PSYCHOSPIRITUAL MATTERS

From a psychiatric perspective there is a wealth of evidence of a condition that was once known as Multiple Personality Disorder and is now generally termed Dissociative Identity Disorder. Those diagnosed with this condition, according to psychiatrist Colin Ross, "have other people inside. The alter personalities may differ in name, age, gender, hair color, or any other imaginable attribute."[9] Dissociative Identity Disorder, says Ross, "is usually linked to severe childhood trauma, which can involve any combination of physical, sexual, and emotional abuse, neglect, loss of primary caretakers, and family violence and chaos."[10] Psychiatrists have long reported encountering mental health patients who manifest the presence of different personalities in one person. A typical narrative of such patients recounts childhood trauma, which resulted in the emergence within them of different (alter) personalities able, as it were, to deal with the particular traumatic occurrences they were experiencing at the time. The process of 'dissociation' (sometimes termed "fragmentation" or "splitting") results in the discernible presence of a fully or partially formed different personality who remains alive and active for differing lengths of time. Ross explains, "One alter personality, A, may be aware of another personality, B, or may have complete amnesia for periods when B is in executive control of the body."[11]

In psychiatric treatment of Dissociative Identity Disorder, what is sought is an integration or at least peaceful co-existence of the alter personalities within the one body. As Ross puts it, "all the different people or souls are fragmented aspects of a single person. In a successfully treated case, the fragments are integrated into a unified single identity."[12] As such, in psychiatric terms, alter-personalities are not 'demons' or evil spirits to be expelled but rather are broken-off aspects of one's wholeness needing to be re-integrated into ones being.

---

9. Ross, "Dissociative Identity Disorder," 147–161.
10. Ibid., 147.
11. Ibid., 148.
12. Ibid., 149.

## AFRICAN VIEWS OF PERSONHOOD

As a contextually relevant exercise, I would make references to the understanding of two West African ethnic communities and their views of human personhood, namely the Gã people of South Eastern Ghana, and the Akan of Ghana and La Côte D'Ivoire.

The Gã people and the Akans are examples of the many West African and, indeed, other African peoples who have a view of human beings as consisting of multiple 'souls.' Of Akans, there are more than fifteen sub-groupings, the Asante and the Fante being among the most well-known.

Akans believe that each human person, at his or her conception, receives specific physical and spiritual elements from the Creator (Onyame), mother, father, and the earth. These are *okra, sunsum, mogya,* and *nipadua*. Of these, the first two are spiritual and the latter two physical. What is of importance in this discussion is that Akans understand that there are two "spiritual entities" or "souls" present in any human being. The *okra*, (or simply *kra*), is regarded as the principle of life, the vital force without which life cannot exist. This each person receives, directly from God prior to birth, and is in a unique and personal relation with the Creator. The *kra*, which has been described as the 'life-soul,'[13] is the bearer of the person's *nkrabea* (destiny), which is negotiated with the Creator prior to birth. It, thus, is the being within a person, which has a sense of one's life-purpose or goals. The *sunsum* is the spiritual being which accounts for the character, disposition and intellectual characteristics of a person. *Sunsum* is spoken of as the "individual soul,"[14] "ego, personality, character,"[15] "personal soul,"[16] "the power that sustains a person's character or individuality,"[17] "essence of being, its intrinsic activating principle."[18]

In contrast to the *kra*, which is always constant and unchangeable, (although it can feel shame, disgrace, and can withdraw or temporarily leave the person), the *sunsum* is subject to change for it can be trained from a state of being "light" to one of being "heavy" by which state is implied the ability to repel evil spiritual beings, as well as 'strength of personality,' or

---

13. Taylor, *The Primal Vision*.
14. Ibid.
15. Busia, *The Position of the Chief*.
16. Meyerowitz in Acolaste, *For Freedom or Bondage*, 62–63.
17. Danquah in Acolaste, *For Freedom or Bondage*, 62–63.
18. Minkus Acolaste, *For Freedom or Bondage*, 62–63.

self-confidence. It is commonly believed that the *susnsum* is linked with the moral quality of a person's behavior, and is able to leave the body during sleep.

These two "souls" inhabit the body of every individual person. They are distinguishable and account for different characteristics of the person. These inner, spiritual, entities are the motivational, moral agents and enlivening beings that give each individual person their distinctive character and personhood.

According to Gã understanding, a human being (gbɔmɔ adesa) is a compound being consisting of three distinct constituents, namely *kla*, *susuma*, and *gbɔmɔtso*. *Kla* and *susuma* are the two spiritual or immaterial 'souls' of a person whilst *gbɔmɔtso* (literally "person-tree") is the physical body. *Susuma* corresponds to the inner soul or personality of a human being. The *susuma* is understood to be able to leave the body during sleep and is the active being in dreams. A *susuma* is not always conscious even when a person is awake. A person, it is said, may at times not know what their *susuma* wants. Moreover, it is often said that the *susuma* "knows more than the person himself knows" or "is wiser than the person" it indwells. John Taylor has described this as "the transcendent-soul" within a person.[19]

*Kla* corresponds to the 'self' and, although like the *susuma* it is invisible, it is believed to have bodily organs that are associated with those of the visible body. The *kla* is the enlivening being within a person. If the *kla* leaves the body life ends. Human life is only possible when the *susuma* and the *kla* are harmoniously conjoined with the body. In addition to this, the *kla* is the bearer of *gbeshi* (fate, luck, or life-script). Like the English word fate, *gbeshi* usually has an unpleasant connotation. *Gbeshi* is often personified, but is always seen as external to its owner and not part of a person's constitutive make up. Thus, as anthropologist Margaret Field noted, Gã people do distinguish between the "premeditated wickedness of a bad-hearted person and the unfortunate wickedness of a well-meaning person afflicted by an unruly gbeshi." [20]

Thus, Gã people, like Akans, also understand humanity to be 'multiply-souled.' These "souls" are an integral part of a person's humanity and, indeed, their strength as persons. Any attempt to deprive a person of any of these constitutive parts of their beings would be seen as evil, and any

---

19. Ibid., 62–63.
20. Field, *Religion and Medicine*, 95.

practitioners of arts directed at expelling parts of a person's life-force would result in these practitioners being seen as 'witches.'

On the contrary, the work of priests or healers in this African-world-sense is that of enhancing the "vital life force," as Magesa would term it.[21] This may include the removal, or dispelling, of evil spiritual entities through the engagement of potent rituals, but they would also entail utilizing all means necessary to strengthen, fortify, and integrate the spiritual power of the individual within their communal setting. The human person's soul or ego strengths need integrating and empowering not removal. It is only debilitating external occupants of inner space that are to be dislodged. This calls for diagnosis and discernment.

## DISCERNMENT AND DIAGNOSIS

In caring for the sick in Africa, and among persons of African descent worldwide, in order to secure the best outcomes, medical and psychiatric diagnosis need to be augmented with spiritual discernment. It is important that these two go hand-in-hand. Pastors and religious workers have a contribution to make to the wellbeing of people, as do medical and psychiatrically trained personnel. Pastors and spiritual caregivers need to realize that not all problems are of a spiritual nature. Doctors and psychiatrists need to recognize that not all problems come from the physical or emotional makeup of a person. Both sets of practitioners also must realize that some conditions are a result of BOTH physical/emotional and spiritual causes. As such, it is imperative that healing practitioners engage in respectful teamwork in which spiritual discernment is not ridiculed, nor are physical or psychological diagnoses considered unimportant.

People engaged in ministries of deliverance are well advised to seek out and work with medical and mental health practitioners. In such circumstances, it becomes possible to cooperate and collaborate in discovering the often multiple causation that underlies the symptomatology that a patient manifests.

---

21. Magesa, *African Religion*.

## EXORCISM, DELIVERANCE, AND HEALTHCARE DELIVERY

The mutual suspicions that held sway between medical and religious approaches to wellness, for centuries, have begun to give way to greater collaboration between practitioners of these disciplines. Psychiatrist Colin Ross, who has engaged in decades of research on practices of exorcism in various parts of the world, offers the following conclusion,

> "My conclusion from my clinical experience and research is that exorcism is a universal, time-honored therapeutic ritual. The utility and outcome of exorcism rituals for dissociative identity disorder cannot help us solve spiritual problems. Used in an empowering, empathic, and restrained manner, it can be very helpful as a therapeutic process. Used in an invasive, violent, dictatorial fashion, it can be destructive. The problem is not with exorcism as such, but rather with the way it is carried out. This is equally true of all other techniques used in psychotherapy."[22]

Professional Christian counselor and seminary professor Dennis Bull argues for what he terms a "phenomenological approach," which appears to me to have much merit. Bull, who has carefully researched the subject, avers that, "exorcism can be viewed as a cognitive behavioral approach to dealing with patients' distress in a culturally sensitive manner."[23] With reference to earlier studies[24] Bull demonstrates that exorcisms may actually be harmful "when there is anything less than full and complete permission from the patient."[25] Counselors of any persuasion "should not unilaterally conclude that a person's symptoms are the result of demonic activity without fully discussing this with the person."[26] Bull documents, "very deleterious results from exorcisms conducted without the greatest care taken to insure the cooperation of the person in the process and with those exorcisms done in ignorance of how dissociative phenomenon (sic) present symptomatically."[27]

---

22. Ross, *Trauma Model*, 158.
23. Bull, "A Phenomenological Model." 137.
24. Bowman, 1997; Fraser, 1993b
25. Ibid., 137.
26. ibid.,
27. Ibid.,138.

Instead, he is favorably disposed to the use of a "psycho-spiritual method that reduces psychological distress and moves patients toward integration of their fractured psyches."[28]

Bull recommends that psychological explorations and explanations should precede spiritual warfare. This is because, as he puts it, "fully developed alter personalities can appear as demons to the uninformed and inexperienced."[29]

In this regard, pastoral theologian Esther Acolatse writes, "sticking the name of a demon on a complex, multifaceted problem, may give the illusion of understanding, and may be understandable in a context in which there are a limited number of therapists, psychiatrists, and social workers, but it falls woefully short of addressing the root issues that people really face."[30]

Likewise, Bull appeals to those practitioners of healing "with an anti-supernatural worldview or those who view the reality of demons with skepticism. . . . to consider the positive results that have been reported in the literature, and to consider taking an appropriate phenomenological and culture-bound approach to Christian patients and to consider using a patient's spiritual resources as an ally in healing."[31]

## GUIDELINES FOR DELIVERANCE MINISTRIES

### Total Care

1. Develop healthy relationships with mental health professionals such as psychiatrists, clinical social workers, psychologists, and psychotherapists. Mutual interaction and teamwork in the treatment of patients is more beneficial than competition and distrust. The wellbeing of the patient needs to be paramount. Medical care is an ally, not an enemy, in the quest for total well-being for all people.

2. Take great care before diagnosing or classifying someone as "demon possessed." Hasty diagnoses are frequently wrongheaded.

---

28. Ibid.
29. Ibid., 138.
30. Acolatse, *For Freedom or Bondage*. 191.
31. Ibid.

3. Begin with the physiological, social, and psychological. Only after having exhausted these categories do you then proceed to the more spiritual.

4. Recognize that for any distressing condition there may be multiple causes. Take time to listen carefully to the ill person's story, paying attention to the intricacies of their experience. Many forces may be at work, not all of them spiritual.

5. Remember that not all "personalities" manifest in a person are to be removed. You may be confronting strong aspects of a healthy person that have enabled the sufferer to overcome trauma in their past. These aspects of their complex selfhood need to be strengthened not removed.

6. Where there are no forces to be expelled, harmonious integration of the various identified "selves" is what needs to be prayed for and sought.

7. Having carefully determined the presence of a spiritual element needing to be removed, seek the consent and active collaboration of the patient through respectful interaction with the patient before a prayer of deliverance.

8. Never 'demonize' the patient. Even if demons are present realize that the patient is NOT the demon.

9. Never resort to physical violence or manipulation. Under no circumstances should patients be subjected to physical, emotional, or social abuse. Some uninformed pastors have been known to try to physically beat the 'demonized' person, or else to starve them in the effort to rid them of demonic influence. Not only is it morally reprehensible and unbiblical to physically assault a patient, it is exceedingly harmful and may result in physical harm or even death. Always maintain respect for the patient's rights as a human being.

10. Put in place social, psychological, and spiritual after-care modalities. Be sure that the patient is not isolated or neglected after the procedure has been completed. The need for social and psychological after-care is especially acute following a deliverance session.

# Contributors

## EMMANUEL Y. LARTEY, PhD

Currently L. Bevel Jones III Professor of Pastoral Theology, Care and Counseling
Candler School of Theology, Emory University in Atlanta, GA, USA
Formerly Senior Lecturer in Pastoral Studies and Practical Theology
Department of Theology, University of Birmingham, UK
Professor of Pastoral Theology and Care at Columbia Theological Seminary, Decatur, Georgia
Chairperson of the British and Irish Association for Practical Theology
President of the International Council for Pastoral Care and Counseling

He is co-Editor of the Journal of Pastoral Theology. In addition to 25 chapters in edited volumes and over 16 articles in peer-reviewed journals, Lartey's single authored book publications include *Pastoral Counseling in Intercultural Perspective*, (1987); *In Living Color: an Intercultural Approach to Pastoral Care and Counseling*, (1997/2003) and *Pastoral Theology in an Intercultural World* (2006). His latest book is titled *Postcolonializing God: An African practical theology* (2013).

## TAPIWA N. MUCHERERA, PhD

Professor of Pastoral Care and Counseling, Asbury Theological Seminary
Ordained Elder of United Methodist Church
Member in full connection with the Zimbabwe West Annual Conference
Affiliated Member of the Florida United Methodist Annual Conference

Board of Ordained Ministry of the Florida United Methodist Annual Conference

ACPE National Board as a National Seminary Representative

He has served several churches in Zimbabwe, Chicago, Iowa, Denver, and Kentucky.

He is author of three books:*Glimmers of Hope* (2013), *Meet me at the Palaver* (2009), *Pastoral Care from a Third World Perspective* (2001), 2005). He has chapters in Anne E. Streaty Wimberly, *Keep it Real: Working with Today's Black Youth* (2005), and Stephen Madigen, *Therapy from Outside In*, (2004).

## ANNE KIOME GATOBU, PhD

*Associate Professor of Pastoral Care & Counseling*, Asbury Theology Seminary

Completed a four-year term as Dean of the School of Practical Theology

Ordained Elder, United Methodist Church

Great Plains Annual Conference, United Methodist Church

Experienced as a pastoral psychotherapist and case manager in trauma and family counseling, Gatobu founded and established FOWCUS-Kenya—a nonprofit, US-based ministry to orphaned children and women in Kenya—and has organized mission trips to Africa since 2004. She is the author of *Female Identity Formation and Response to Intimate Trauma: A Case Study of Domestic Violence in Kenya*.

## ESTHER ACOLASTE, PhD

Assistant Professor of the Practice of Theology and World Christianity at Duke Divinity School

Served the global church in several capacities for many years both in her native Ghana and through her denomination, the Presbyterian Church (USA.)

She is the author of *For Freedom or Bondage: A critique of African Pastoral Practices* and the forthcoming *Fleeing from the Spirit? Biblical Realism and the Demands of Contextual Theology* (Wm. B. Eerdmans). Recent articles address spiritual and psychological factors in care at the end of life and include "Embracing and Resisting Death: A Theology of Justice and Hope for Care at the End of Life" in *Living Faithfully Dying Well: Christian Practices of Care at the End of Life*, and "God as Good-Enough Mother: The Development of Hope in Job" in *Journal of Pastoral Theology*.

## M. FULGENCE NYENGELE, PhD

Professor of Pastoral Care and Counseling, Methodist Theological School in Ohio

William A. Chryst Chair, Methodist Theological School in Ohio

Director of the M.A. in Counseling Ministries program

Ordained elder in the United Methodist Church in the Congo

Affiliate member of the West Ohio Conference of the United Methodist Church

Member of the American Counseling Association

Member of the American Association of Pastoral Counselors

He is the author of several articles and a book, including "Cultivating *Ubuntu*: An African Postcolonial Pastoral Theological Engagement with Positive Psychology," *Journal Pastoral Theology*(2014); "African Spirituality and the Wesleyan Spirit: Implications for Spiritual Formation in a Multicultural Church and Culturally Pluralistic World, (Oxford Institute, 2013), "Gender Injustice and Pastoral Care in an African Context: Perichoresis as a Transformative Theological Resource," *Journal of Theology* 110 (2006); *African Women's Theology, Gender Relations and Family Systems Theory: Pastoral Theological Considerations and Guidelines for Care and Counseling* (Peter Lang, 2004).

## MAZVITA MACHINGA PhD

Pastoral Psychotherapist, Zimbabwe

CONTRIBUTORS

PhD in Pastoral Psychotherapy, Claremont School of Theology

Masters in Practical Theology-Pastoral Care and Counseling, USA

Masters of Science in Psychology, UK

Mental health consultant, Mental Health First Aid Certified Instructor

Worked in mental health and counseling interventions and services to at-risk children, vulnerable families and communities

## MAAKE J. MASANGO, PhD

Emeritus Professor in Practical Theology at the University of Pretoria. SA.

Member of the World Council of Churches and the World Alliance of Reform Churches

Moderator of his General Synod in the Uniting Presbyterian Church of South Africa

Executive member of the All Africa Conference of Churches

Vice-president of the South African Council of Churches

President of Urban Rural Mission (International)

Vice-president of the Society for Practical Theology in South Africa

Member of Societas Homiletica, the International Society for Homiletics

Executive member of Peace for Life in Asia

Member of Georgia Association of Pastoral Care

Psychotherapist certified by the American Association of Pastoral Care

His fields of specialization are Practical Theology based on the themes of violence and abuse of marginalized people. Masango is a prolific writer with several publications (Books and Academic articles). As vice-president of the SA Council of Churches he addressed the Swedish Government on the issue of arms and state of the nation of South Africa. He received several awards, including: A Fulbright Scholarship (shared with Dr Drew Smith) in 2008; Peace award by Mar Thoma Syrian Orthodox Church of Malabar, India in 2008; A distinguish Service Alumnus Award by Columbia Seminary, USA in 2008; In 1999 he was recognized as Kairos Theologian by the

Institute of Contextual Theology and he was offered Awarded Citizenship by the Mayor of California

# Bibliography

Acolatse, Esther E. *For Freedom or Bondage? A Critique of African Pastoral Practices.* Grand Rapids, MN: William B. Eerdmans, 2014.

Agence France-Press. September 9, 2008; retrieved 9/6/2016. http://www.lapresse.ca/international/200809/19/01-670076-un-ex-employe-de-lonu-juge-pour-viols-sur-mineurs-en-afrique

Alexander, Jeffrey C. ed. "Toward a Theory of Cultural Trauma." In *Cultural Trauma and Collective Identity.* Los Angeles, CA: University of California Press, 2004.

Amanor, Jones Darkwa. "Pentecostalism in Ghana: An African Reformation." In *Cyberjournal for Pentecostal-Charismatic Research.* April 13, 2004. http://www.pctii.org/cyberj/cyberj13/amanor.html

Appiah, Kwame Anthony. *In My Father's House: Africa in the Philosophy of Culture.* New York: Oxford University Press, 1992.

Asamoah-Gyadu, J. Kwabena. *African Charismatics: Current developments within Independent Indigenous Pentecostalism in Ghana.* Leiden: E.J. Brill, 2005.

Auerhahn, N.C. and D. Laub. "Intergenerational Memory of the Holocaust." In *International Handbook of Multigenerational Legacies of Trauma,* Yael Danieli, ed. New York: Plenum, 1998.

Avert. *HIV and AIDS in Zimbabwe.* Aug. 20, 2015. http://www.avert.org/hiv-aids-zimbabwe.htm

Basham, Don. *Deliver Us From Evil.* Grand Rapids, MI: Chosen/Baker, 2014.

Bastien, Betty, et al. "Healing the Impact of Colonization, Genocide, and Racism on Indigenous Populations." In *The Psychological Impact of War Trauma on Civilians: An International Perspective,* ed. Stanley Krippner and Teresa M. McIntyre. Westport, Connecticut: Praeger, 2003.

Becker, David. *Dealing with the Consequences of Organized Violence in Trauma Work.* Berghof Research Center for Constructive Conflict Management, 2004.

Bhengu, M. J. *Ubuntu: The Essence of Democracy.* Cape Town, South Africa: Novalis, 1996.

Bloom, Sandra. *Creating Sanctuary: Toward an Evolution of Sane Societies.* New York: Routledge, 1997.

Bojuwoye, Olaniyi. *Traditional Healing Practices in Southern Africa*. In *Moodley and West: Integrating Traditional Practices into Counseling and Psychotherapy*. Thousand Oaks: Sage, Series 22, 2005.

Brave Heart, Maria Yellow Horse, and Deschenie, Tina. "Historical Trauma and Post-Colonial Stress in American Indian Populations." In *Tribal College Journal of American Indian Higher Education*. Vol. 17, No.3, Spring, 2006.

"'Breaking the Silence' on Congo," *Faith in Action: News and Views from the United Methodist Board of Church and Society*. October 6, 2008.

Broodryk, J. *Ubuntu: Life Lessons From Africa*. Pretoria: Ubuntu School of Philosophy, 2004.

Bull, Dennis L. "A Phenomenological Model of Therapeutic Exorcism for Dissociative Identity Disorder." In *Journal of Psychology and Theology*. Vol. 29, No. 2, 2009.

Busia, Kofi A. *The Position of the Chief in the Modern Political System of Ashanti: A Study of the Influence of Contemporary Social Changes on Ashanti Political Institutions*. Oxford: Oxford University Press, 1951.

Cannon, Nona H. *Roots of Violence, Seeds of Peace in People, Families and Society*. San Diego, CA: Miclearoy, 1996.

Carroll, Jackson. *God's Potters: Pastoral Leadership and the Shaping of Congregations*. Grand Rapids, MI: Eerdmans, 2006.

Cerulli, Catherine, et al. "Maternal Intergenerational Transmission of Childhood Multitype Maltreatment." In *Journal of Aggression, Maltraitement and Trauma*. 20, 2011.

Chimedza, P. *Let's do SARS act on HIV, AIDS: HIV and Mandatory Testing*. May 21, 2006. In *The Sunday Mail*, pchimedza@hotmail.com

"Colonialism." In *Stanford Encyclopedia of Philosophy*. At http://plato.stanford.edu, retrieved 7/25/2016.

Cook, Christopher C.H. ed. *Spirituality, Theology and Mental Health: Multidisciplinary perspectives*. London: SCM Press, 2013.

Cross, W.E. *A Two-factor Theory of Black Identity: Implications for the Study of Identity Development in Minority Children*. In *Children's Ethnic socialization, Pluralism and Development*. Newbury Park, CA: Sage, 1987.

Daniels, Anthony. "Western Perceptions of Postcolonial Violence in Africa." In *Political Violence: Belief, Behavior, and Legitimation*. New York: Palgrave Macmillan, 2008.

David, E.J.R. *Filipino/American Postcolonial Psychology: Oppression, Colonial Mentality, and Decolonization*. Bloomington, IN: AuthorHouse, 2011.

DeGruy, Joy. *Post Traumatic Slave Syndrome: America's Legacy of Enduring Injury and Healing*. Milwaukie, MN: Uptone Press, 2005.

Demeestere, Matthieu. Un Ex-Exemployé de l' ONU Jugé pour Viols sur Mineures en Afrique. In *Agence France-Press*, September 9, 2008; retrieved 9/6/2016. http://www.lapresse.ca/international/200809/19/01-670076-un-ex-employe-de-lonu-juge-pour-viols-sur-mineurs-en-afrique

Dickson, Kwesi A. *Theology in Africa*. Maryknoll, NY: Orbis, 1984.

Dirlik, Arif. "Rethinking Colonialism: Globalization, Postcolonialism, and the Nation." In *Interventions*. Vol. 4(3), 2002.

Donkor, A. E. *African Spirituality: On Becoming Ancestors*. Trenton, New Jersey: Africa World, 1997.

Dube, Musa, Adikira. "Four Hearts Joined Together." In *Phiri, Isabel and Nadar Sarojini, African Women, Religion, and Health*. New York: Orbis Books, 2006.

# Bibliography

Duff, Nancy J. "Recovering Lamentation as a Practice in the Church." In *Lament*, Louisville: Westminster John Knox, 2005.

Dummett, Mark. "King Leopold's Legacy of DR Congo Violence." In *BBC News* February, 2004; retrieved 7/15/2016 http://newsbbc.co.uk/2/hi/africa/3516965.stm

Duran, Edwardo. *Native American Postcolonial Psychology*. New York: State University of New York Press, 1995.

Easton Bible Dictionary, http://www.biblestudytools.com/dictionary/bethesda/

Elkins, Caroline. *Imperial Reckoning: The Untold Story of Britain's Gulag in Kenya*. New York: Henry Hold and Company, 2005.

Ellingsen, Mark. "Luther's concept of the Ministry: The Creative Tension." In *Word & World* 1.4, 1981.

Erickson, Kai. *A New Species of Trouble: The Human Experience of Modern Disasters*. New York: Norton, 1994.

ESV. *The Holy Bible*. evsbible.org.

Field, Margaret J. *Religion and Medicine of the Ga People*. London: Oxford University Press, 1937.

Freedman, J. and G. Combs. *Narrative Therapy: The Social Construction of Preferred Realities*. New York: W. W. Norton & Company, 1996.

Friedman, Edwin. "Bowen Therapy." In *Handbook of Family Therapy*. Volume 2, New York: Brunner/Mazel, 1991.

Fuller, Rogers Dalene C. *Pastoral Care for Post-Traumatic Stress Disorder: Healing the Shattered Soul*. New York: Haworth Pastoral, 2002.

Galek, Kathleen et.al. "Spiritual Needs: Gender Differences among Professional Spiritual Care Providers." In *The Journal of Pastoral Care and Counseling*. 62, spring–summer 2008, nos. 1–2.

Gerkin, Charles. Cited in Andrew Lester, *Hope in Pastoral Care and Counseling*. Louisville: Westminster John Knox, 1995.

"Ghanaian Pastor Kicks and Steps on the Stomach of a Pregnant Woman." *Sahara Reporters*. December 5, 2014. http://saharareporters.com/2014/12/05/video-ghanaian-pastor-kicks-and-steps-stomach-pregnant-woman.

Gilroy, Paul. *Postcolonial Melancholia*. New York: Columbia University Press, 2004.

Graham, L. K. Healing. In, *Dictionary of Pastoral Care and Counseling*. Nashville, TN: Abingdon, 1990.

Gunda, Masiiwa Ragies. "Christianity, Traditional Religion, and Healing in Zimbabwe Exploring the Dimensions and Dynamics of Healing Among the Shona." In *Svensk missionstidskrift*. 95.3, 2007.

———. "Jesus Christ: Homosexuality and Masculinity in African Christianity: Reading Luke 10:1–12." Exchange 42 (2013).

Harvery, Diane. "Intergenerational Transmission of Trauma from Holocaust Survivors to their Children." At http://www.thetrustingheart.com retrieved 11/0/2015.

Herman Judith. *Trauma and Recovery: The Aftermath of Violence from Domestic Abuse to Political Violence*. New York: Basic Books, 1992.

Herman, Susan. "Foreword." In *Trauma Counseling: Theories and Interventions*. New York: Springer Publications Company, 2012.

HIPPA http://www.hhs.gov/ocr/privacy/hipaa/faq/personal_representatives_and_minors/230.html(http://www.hhs.gov/ocr/privacy).

Hochschild, Adam. "Introduction." In Jules Marchal, *Lord Leverhulme's Ghosts: Colonial Exploitation in the Congo*. London: Verso, 2008.

# Bibliography

———. *King Leopold's Ghost: A Story of Greed, Terror, and Heroism in Colonial Africa.* New York: Houghton Mifflin Company, 1998.

Howe, Stephen. "Internal Decolonization? British Politics since Thatcher as Post-colonial Trauma." In *Twentieth Century British History.* Vol. 14, No.3, 2003.

"Installation of an Asantehene." In *Ghana, Culture, Politics.* http://ghanaculturepolitics.com/installation-of-an-asantehene/ January 18, 2015.

Joy, Charles R., ed. *Albert Schweitzer: An Anthology.* Boston: Beacon, 1965 [1947].

Kamwaria, A. and M. Katola. "The Role of African Tradition, Culture and World-view in the Context of Post War Healing Among the Dinka Community of Southern Sudan." In *International Journal of Humanities and Social Sciences.* Vol 2 No. 21, Nov 12.

Kasambala, Amon Eddie. "The Impact of an African Spirituality"

Kellerman, Nathan P.F. "Transmission of Holocaust Trauma." In *National Israeli Center for Psychosocial Support of Survivors of the Holocaust and the Second Generation* Jerusalem, Israel: retrieved 11/24/2012.

"Key Terms in Post-Colonial Theory." At http://www3.dbu.edu/mitchell/postcold.htm retrieved 7/25/2016.

Kiome-Gatobu, Anne. *Female Identity Formation and Response to Intimate Trauma.* Eugene, OR: Pickwick Publications, 2013.

Lederach, John Paul. *Building Peace: Sustainable Reconciliation in Divided Societies.* Washington, DC: United States Institute of Peace, 1999.

———. *When Blood and Bones Cry Out: Journeys Through the Soundscape of Healing and Reconciliation.* Oxford: Oxford University Press, 2010.

Lesley, Gill. "War and Peace in Colombia." In *Social Analysis* 52:2. Summer 2008.

Lester, Andrew. *Hope in Pastoral Care and Counseling.* Louisville, KY: Westminster John Knox, 1995.

Leveton, Eva. *Healing Collective Trauma Using Sociodrama and Drama Therapy.* New York: Springer Publishing Company, 2010.

Likaka, Osumaka. *Naming Colonialism: History and Collective Memory in the Congo 1870–1960.* Madison, WI: University of Wisconsin, 2009.

Lindsell, H. *Harper Study Bible: The Holy Bible.* Grand Rapids, MI: Zondervan, 1980.

Kappen, S. *Spirituality In The New Age of Colonialism.* London: Duquce and Gutierrez and the Institutional Crisis, 1994.

Kludze, A. and P. Kodzo. *Chieftaincy in Ghana.* Lanham, MD: Austin & Winfield, 2000.

Koka, K. D. *Ubuntu: A People's Humanness.* Pretoria: Ubuntu School of Philosophy, 1999.

Kourie, C. and L. Kretzschmar. *Christian Spirituality in South Africa.* Pietermaritzburg: Cluster, 2000.

Kornfeld, Margaret. *Cultivating Wholeness: A Guide to Care and Counseling in Faith Communities.* New York: Continuum, 2008.

Machinga, Mazvita. "Pastoral Care in Post-violence Situations: Tending to the Visible and Invisible Wounds of Survivors in Three Communities in Manicaland Province of Zimbabwe." In *Dissertation.* Claremont School of Theology, 2012.

Magesa, Laurenti. *African Religion: The Moral Traditions of Abundant Life.* Maryknoll, NY: Orbis, 1997.

Mageza, L. *African Religion: The Moral Traditions of Abundant Life.* New York: Orbis, 1997.

Majembe, Pastory M. *A Study to Identify Current Theologies and Praxis for Divorcee in Tanzania's Evangelical/Pentecostal Churches in the Quest for a Redemptive Ministry.* DMin Dissertation, 2013.

Marchal, Jules. *Lord Leverhulme's Ghosts: Colonial Exploitation in the Congo.* London: Verso, 2008.
———. *L'Histoire du Congo* 1910–1945. Tome 1, Borgloon: Editions Paula Bellings, 1999.
———. *Morel Contre Leopold II: L'Histoire du Congo 1900–1910.* Vol. 2, Paris: L'Harmattan, 1996.
Marshall, Ruth. *Political Spiritualities: The Pentecostal Revolution in Nigeria.* Chicago: University of Chicago Press, 2009.
Mbigi, L. and J. Maree. *Ubuntu: The Spirit of African Transformation Management.* Pretoria: Knowledge Resources, 1995.
Mbiti, S. J. *Concepts of God in Africa.* New York: Praeger, 1970.
———. *Introduction to African Religion.* Nairobi: Hennemann, 1977.
———. *African Religion and Philosophy.* Oxford: Hennemann. 1990.
McCaskie, T. C. *Asante, Kingdom of Gold: Essays in the History of an African Culture.* Durham, NC: Carolina Academic, 2015.
Messer, Don. Interview 8-31-2016
Mijares, Sharon and Gurucharan Singh Khalsa. *The Psychospiritual Clinician's Handbook: Alternative methods for understanding and treating mental disorders.* Oxford: Haworth, 2005.
Miller, Laurence. Psychological Interventions for Terroristic Trauma: Symptoms, Syndromes, and Treatment Strategies. In *Psychotherapy:Theory/Research/Practice/Training.* Vol. 39. No. 4, 2002.
Mianda, Gertrude. "Colonialism, Education, and Gender Relations in the Belgian Congo: The *Evolué* Case." In *Women in African Colonial Histories.* Bloomington: Indiana University Press, 2002.
Mims, Sekou, Larry Higginbottom, and Omar Reid. *Post Traumatic Slavery Disorder.* Dorchester, MA: Pyramid Builders.
Mligo, Shabani Elia. *Elements of African Traditional Religion: A textbook for students of comparative religion.* Oregon: Wipsandstock, 2013.
Morgan, Alice. *What Is Narrative Therapy?* Adelaide: Dulwich Centre Publications, 2000.
Morten, G, and D. R. Atkinson. Minority Identity Development and Preference for Counselor Race. In *Journal of Negro Education,* 52, 1983.
Mucherera, Tapiwa N. *Meet me at the Palaver, Narrative Pastoral Counseling in Postcolonial Contexts.* Eugene, OR: Cascade Books, 2009.
———. *Pastoral Care From a Third World Perspective: A Pastoral Theology of Care from an Urban Contemporary Shona in Zimbabwe.* New York: Peter Lang, 2005.
Mukwege, Denis. "Tracing the Source of 'Conflict Minerals.'" In *The New York Times.* April 22, 2015.
Naitore, Nthurima. Interview. 8-31-2016
Nandy, Ashis. *The Intimate Enemy: Loss and Recovery of Self Under Colonialism.* 2nd. edition New York: Oxford University Press, 2009.
Ndaywell a Nziem, Isidore. *Histoire Generale du Congo: De l'Heritage Ancien a la Republique Democratic du Congo.* Paris: Duculot, 1998.
Nichols, M. and R. Shwartz. *Family Therapy: Concepts and Methods.* 8th or 9th Ed. Boston: Allyn & Bacon, 2010.
NIV, https://www.biblegateway.com/passage/?search=Ezekiel%2034:1-24
Nolan, A. *Biblical Spirituality.* Springs: The Order of Preachers of South Africa, 1982.
NRSV, *The Holy Bible.* Oxford, NY: University Press, 1989.

# Bibliography

Nzongola-Ntalaja, Georges. *The Congo from Leopold to Kabila: A People's History*. London: Zed Books, 2002.

O'Dea, James and Judith Thompson. "Social Healing for a Fractured World." In *Shift* http://noetic.org/library/publication-articles/social-healing-fractured-world/ Issue 7, June-August, 2005, accessed November 3, 2011.

Opoku, Kofi Asare. "The West Through African Eyes." In *In the Spirit of Christ: One Humanity, One Struggle One Hope*. Lathonia, GA: SPC/ Third World Literature, 1994.

Olupona, J. K. *African Traditional Religion in Contemporary Society*. Minnesota: Paragon House, 1991.

———. *African Spirituality: Forms and Meanings and Expressions*. New York: Herder & Herder, 2000.

Osnes, Gry. "Succession and Authority: A Case Study of an African Family Business and a Clan Chief." In *International Journal of Cross Cultural Management*. 11.2, 2011.

Pakenham, Thomas. *The Scramble for Africa: White Man's Conquest of the Dark Continent from 1876 to 1912*. New York: Perennial, 1991/2003.

"Pastor Orders Women to Strip." In *This is Africa*. November 21, 2014. https://www.google.com/search?q=south+african+pastor+orders+congregation+to+strip&ie=utf-8&oe=utf-8

Pinderhughes, Alaine. "The Multigenerational Transmission of Loss and Trauma: The African American Experience." In *Living Beyond Loss: Death in the Family*. New York: W.W. Norton & Company, 2004.

Pobee John S. "African Instituted (Independent) Churches." In *Dictionary of the Ecumenical Movement*. Geneva: World Council of Churches, 2002.

———. *Toward an African Theology*. Nashville: Abingdon, 1979.

Rapadas, Juan M. "Transmission of Violence: The Legacy of Colonialism in Guam and the Path to Peace." In *Journal of Pacific Rim Psychology*. Volume 1, Issue 2.

Rattary R. S. *Ashanti Law and Constitution*. Oxford: Clarendon Press, 1969 [1929].

Renton, David, David Seddon, and Leo Zeilig. *The Congo: Plunder and Resistance*. New York: Zed Books, 2007.

Roes, Aldwin. "Towards a History of Mass Violence in the Etat Indépendent du Congo 1885–1908." In *South African Historical Journal*. 62 (4).

Ross, Colin. *Trauma Model Therapy*. Richardson, TX: Manitou Communications, 2009.

Rowlands, Allison. "Trauma Counseling." In *Handbook of International Social Work: Human Rights, Development, and the Global Profession*. New York: Oxford University Press, 2012.

Saul, Jack. *Collective Trauma, Collective Healing: Promoting Community Resilience in the Aftermath of Disaster*. New York: Routledge, 2014.

Savoy, P. *The Best of African Folklore*. Cape Town: Struik, 1988.

Setiloane, G M. *African Theology*. Johannesburg: Skotaville, 1986.

Smelser, Neil J. "Psychological Trauma and Cultural Trauma." In *Cultural Trauma and Collective Identity*. Berkeley, CA: University of California Press, 2004.

"South African Pastor Tells Congregation to Eat Grass to Be Closer to God." https://www.youtube.com/watch?v=bHT1Me3VYMs

Spaas, Lieve. *How Belgium Colonized the Mind of the Congo*. Lewiston, NY: Edwin Mellen, 2007.

Taiwo, Olufemi. *How Colonialism Preempted Modernity in Africa*. Bloomington and Indianapolis: Indiana University Press.

Taylor, John V. *The Primal Vision*. London: SCM Press, 1963.

# Bibliography

The New Oxford American Dictionary, (Online).
Tshitungu, Antoine. "Colonial Memories in Belgian and Congolese Literature." In *Belgian Memories*. Yale University Press, 2002.
Wariboko, Nimi. *Nigerian Pentecostalism*. Rochester, NY: University of Rochester Press, 2014.
Watkins, Ali Caroll. *Survival and Liberation*. St. Louis, MO: Chalice Press, 1999.
Wimberly, Edward P. *Pastoral Care in the Black Church*. Nashville: Abingdon, 1979.
———. *Counseling African American Marriages and Families*. Louisville, Ky: Westminster John Knox, 1997.
Wimberly and Mucherera. "Re-villaging." In *Fourth Congress of the African Association of Pastoral Studies and Counseling*. Yaounde Cameroon, July 27, 2001.
Wink, Walter. *Violence and Nonviolence in South Africa: Jesus' Third Way*. BC, Canada: New Society, 1987.

www.ingramcontent.com/pod-product-compliance
Lightning Source LLC
Chambersburg PA
CBHW072151160426
43197CB00012B/2341